AMERICA'S
ENGINEERED
DECLINE

BY
WILLIAM NORMAN GRIGG

THE JOHN BIRCH SOCIETY
Appleton, Wisconsin

First Printing, April 2004
Second Printing, August 2004

Published by
The John Birch Society
Post Office Box 8040
Appleton, Wisconsin 54912
www.jbs.org

Printed in the United States of America
LC Control Number
2004104073
ISBN: 1-881919-10-2

To my Korrin —

"... like gold to an airy thinness beat...
Thy firmness makes my circle just,
and makes me end where I begun."

Contents

Introduction vi

1. Race to the Bottom 1

2. Banishing Businesses 23

3. Amalgamating the Americas 35

4. Caught in the WTO Web 47

5. Electing a New People 63

6. What Can We Do? 91

   Appendix I. Descent into Degeneracy 105

   Appendix II. The Wages of Perpetual War 125

   Endnotes 138

   Index 155

   About the Author 165

Introduction

There are people in the [Bush] administration, and in Mexico, and in Congress, who believe that we should do away with borders entirely. Their ultimate goal is to create this hemispheric "free trade" area consolidating all of North and South America into some kind of "United States of the Americas." ...

This is a legitimate political issue, and it should be discussed and debated openly. Americans — the public at large as much as some of our policymakers — are letting this take place without a frank discussion. We are undergoing a radical change in our national character and social structure, and it shouldn't be allowed to happen without at very least the informed consent of the public. I'm among those who believe that it shouldn't be allowed to happen, period — and I believe that this remains a majority view, which is probably why it's being done by stealth and misdirection.

— Representative Tom Tancredo (R-Colorado).

Proponents of full hemispheric integration — economic and political — have targeted 2005 for the culmination of a sneak attack on the independence of America. Using the misleading bait of promoting prosperity, the powerful globalists supporting this scheme hope to entice our nation into a revolutionary trap — the cleverly misnamed Free Trade Area of the Americas (FTAA).

Designed as an open-ended political process, the FTAA would steadily harmonize America down to the level of the least fortunate in this hemisphere. Yet few Americans have any awareness of where the Free Trade Area of the Americas is intended to take us. And the architects of this revolution have no intention of advertising their aims.

Accordingly, the publication of *America's Engineered Decline* comes as a very welcome event.

Most Americans old enough to discern trends have become nervous about our nation's future. They recognize that our nation is plagued by problems with serious long-term consequences. Out-of-control immigration and manufacturing flight are but two of those problems examined in *America's Engineered Decline*.

Unfortunately, the public doesn't know what to do about its concerns and generally looks to government for solutions. But, despite much posturing by politicians, the problems continue to get worse.

For example, since 9-11, the public has made it particularly clear that it wants government to enforce control of our borders and stem massive immigration. Yet, instead, we now hear of proposals for amnesty and further opening our borders. Why? Because, as William Norman Grigg shows, our government has been marching to a far different drummer than public opinion.

As *America's Engineered Decline* demonstrates, the public's wishes are constantly frustrated because the public doesn't understand its competition for control of our own government. Most of us are busy with our personal affairs and accordingly not well informed about what our government is actually doing. We are prone to accept excuses and assurances from political leaders while the more diligent and better informed competition gets the results.

America's Engineered Decline will help Americans correct that deficiency. It will help them understand the forces and agendas responsible for our nation's decline. But most importantly, Mr. Grigg's exposé offers help in understanding and — we hope — blocking one of the most dangerous milestones in that decline: The Free Trade Area of the Americas.

The accelerated economic devastation and loss of political control promised by our entry into a Free Trade Areas of the Americas agreement would make it very difficult for Americans to reverse course later when they more clearly see the destination. If you love America and want to pass on a legacy of freedom and opportunity to future generations, please read on. Then get others to do so as well.

Most especially, we urge every reader to get involved in an organized drive to activate Congress to stop the FTAA. Defeating the FTAA would deliver a huge setback to the globalists seeking to fasten stifling socialism on the peoples of the world. Similarly, stopping the FTAA would strike a major blow in the longer struggle to restore constitutional government at home and promote freedom — the real basis for prosperity — throughout the world.

Blocking the FTAA is certainly a big challenge, but organized opposition could well carry the day. Let's remember that majorities don't change the course of history. Determined minorities do. Determined minorities can still mobilize the power of public opinion, using the freedoms our Founding Fathers attempted to secure for us.

Because of the urgency and timeliness of the FTAA threat, the publisher has shifted Mr. Grigg's examination of two other significant national threats — moral decline and perpetual war, which have less to do with the FTAA proposal itself — to appendices. Readers who find the main portion of this short book enlightening will be well served to continue reading and discover what else Mr. Grigg has to say about *America's Engineered Decline*.

Tom Gow, Publisher
March 2004

CHAPTER ONE

Race to the Bottom

[T]he elite hated the middle class which challenged them in the name of God-given liberty. And little wonder that this hatred grew deeper as the middle class became stronger and imposed restrictions through which all the people, including the most humble, had the right to rule their own lives and keep the greater part of what they earned for themselves. Clearly, if the elite were to rule again, the middle class had to be destroyed.... For you see the elite of all nations, then as now, were not divided. They were one international class, and worked together and protected each other. But the middle class laughed and said, "We will bind you with the chains of our Constitution, which you must obey also, lest we depose you, for we are now powerful and we are human beings and we wish to be free from your old despotism."
— Taylor Caldwell[1]

What does it do when you take away all these jobs from people who support families, who raise families? ... Manufacturing has been the strength of this country. If we can't make anything here anymore, what does that do? The fabric of this society is falling apart.
— Jim Greathouse, 55, 30-year employee of a Hoover vacuum factory in Canton, Ohio, after losing his job in June 2003[2]

We're basically liquidating our whole middle class, polarizing people on the two extremes, haves and have-nots.... We'll be a third-world country.
— Roger Chastain, president of the Mount Vernon

1

Mills of Greenville, South Carolina[3]

It makes me wonder if there is some merit to the 'con-
spiracy theory' — the idea that all of this is part of a de-
liberate scheme to wipe out the middle class. The mid-
dle class is always a pain in the neck where govern-
ment's concerned. It's where you find most of the peo-
ple who complain about taxes, regulations, and other
policies. If you wipe them out, you just have the ultra-
rich and the poor — a perfect arrangement for a dicta-
torship.

— Jerry Skoff, owner of Badger Tech Metals in
Menomonee, Wisconsin[4]

"We were middle class," lamented former textile worker Jimmy Bennett, before hastily correcting himself:
"We still are." Jimmy and his wife, Verleen, residents of Kannapolis, North Carolina, were among the nearly 6,500 employees of the Pillowtex towel factory who were laid off in early August 2003.

Just two years earlier, the Bennetts had bought a modest
four-bedroom ranch house. After putting in a combined 43 years
at the mill, working part-time jobs, and frugally managing their
money, "we had made it," Jimmy told a *Washington Post* reporter.[5] But their thrift and industry weren't enough to save their
jobs as Pillowtex — like much of America's textile industry —
was deluged by a flood of cheap imports from China.

Now the Bennetts and thousands of Pillowtex employees
found themselves in an economic free-fall, shedding many of
the middle-class amenities to which they had become accus-
tomed. Many were left fending off foreclosures, eviction notices, or car repossessions. Luxuries such as cable television
and cell phones were jettisoned, and soon necessities were in
jeopardy as well: Within weeks of the lay-off, more than 200
former employees had their water turned off.[6]

Kannapolis means "city of looms," and the town's textile mills offered steady employment to several generations. Many, if not most, of those who toiled in the mills had a high school education, supplemented with an admirable work ethic. When the looms fell silent, many of those workers were cresting middle age, with families to support, and mortgages to pay. Some, like the Bennetts, quickly took any available jobs, even those at near-minimum wage. Others tried to find other textile jobs, or similar work in the manufacturing sector, but their prospects were less than encouraging — given the accelerating flight of manufacturing work abroad, particularly to China.

According to Charles Bremer of the American Textile Manufacturers Institute, as textiles from Communist China and Vietnam flood the American market, "People are moving jobs faster than you can count." In 2008, all import quotas on Chinese textiles will be removed. "At that point," predicts Bremer, "the Chinese will completely dominate the market."[7]

Ironically, at least some of the future textile imports from China will probably be produced on looms from Pillowtex's Kannapolis facility — but those looms will be in China, operated by Chinese workers. As thousands of the company's workers scrambled to find new jobs, or to keep creditors at bay, brokers and investors scrambled to carve up the company's remaining assets. The company's looms and other heavy machinery were likely destined for China, Pakistan, or India.[8]

Manufacturing in Decline

The Kannapolis tragedy is merely a small snapshot of the general decline of America's manufacturing economy.

"While hundreds of factories close in any given year," observed the *Wall Street Journal*, "something historic and fundamentally different is occurring now. For manufacturing, this isn't a cyclical downturn. Most of these basic and low-skill factory jobs aren't liable to come back when the economy recovers or when excess capacity around the world dissolves...."

[T]he task of making these [manufactured] goods is increasingly being assumed by more efficient machines and processes. Or they've been transferred to workers who earn less and live in another country.... By some estimates, roughly 1.3 million manufacturing jobs have moved abroad since the beginning of 1992, the bulk in the past three years [2000-2003] to Mexico and East Asia."[9]

In a Labor Day speech in 2003 before union workers in Ohio — a state that shed 160,000 manufacturing jobs between 2000 and 2003[10] — President George W. Bush tried to play up the notion that the job losses reflected increases in productivity, corporate greed and corruption, and the September 11th terrorist attacks.

"What productivity means is that we've got a lot of hard work and we're using new technologies to make people more effective when it comes to the job, and that's important," insisted the president. "You see, in 1979, it took more than 40 hours of labor to make a car, and now it takes 18 hours. We're productive. Our workers are really productive in America."[11]

It's certainly true that advances in technology have dramatically improved American productivity. But the perspective offered by President Bush perversely blames "the most productive workers in the entire world" for the dismal prospects that await them as manufacturing jobs evaporate. Furthermore, there is sound reason to believe that our nation's performance on the productivity front reflects not a healthy, streamlined economy, but the Federal Reserve's success in redefining productivity for political reasons.

"The supposed rise in productivity was the silver lining in the economic cloud of the last three years," wrote *New York Post* economics analyst John Crudele in late 2003. "Fed Chief Alan Greenspan has spoken proudly of it, saying the United States was becoming a more efficient producer of goods. But a slip of a tongue may call the whole productivity miracle into question."

The wayward tongue in question belongs to Senator Robert Bennett (R-Utah), chairman of the Joint Economics Committee. In a television interview, Bennett — apparently unaware of the implications of his comments — offered an off-the-cuff description of the Federal Reserve's Soviet-style redefinition of "productivity" in the mid-1990s:

> If you go back into the '90s and Alan Greenspan's examination of where the economy was, the productivity numbers that he was getting through traditional means all indicated productivity was down. And Greenspan gathered the economists ... and the Fed together and said this cannot be right.... They said, 'We are doing it the way we've always done it, so the numbers have to be right.' And [Greenspan] challenged them and said if you look at the other data they make it very clear that productivity has got to be going up. They went back and recalculated and discovered that their productivity numbers had been wrong for months if not years.[12]

Here's how the process works, according to Crudele: "The Fed Chairman doesn't like an economic statistic, so he tells some lowly economists to take a mulligan and do the calculations over. Amazingly, they discover exactly what the Fed wants them to discover — the politically important productivity miracle."[13]

Thus it's clear that productivity hasn't caused the dramatic reduction in the number of American manufacturing jobs. "Outsourcing" — sending work abroad to be done more cheaply by foreign workers — is a much likelier culprit.

During the summer of 2003, ten plants operated by the Hooker Furniture Corporation were shuttered, leaving hundreds of people from several states unemployed. This was not an austerity measure, since the company's profits had actually increased during recent years — largely because it had started to "outsource" its work to cheaper foreign manufacturers.[14]

"Every time we've asked them to step up, they've done it," commented Hooker CEO Paul Toms of the employees who lost their jobs. "I feel like we've let these folks down, and I don't know what I'd do different.... It's unlike anything I've seen in my 21 years in the industry. A lot of plants have closed, people have been sent home, and it really has come quicker than anybody expected. I think it's hard to say, three, four, five years from now, what this industry will look like domestically."[15]

As with the American textile industry, the U.S. furniture industry has been decimated in uneven competition with low-wage nations like Communist China. The Chinese "have millions of people that they're trying to have employed so it's hard to fault them," Toms opines. "But I think that at some point, this country has to think about what's best for us.... You have industries and examples of predatory pricing. That's the risk we run not just in furniture, but in any industry that we're letting leave this country."[16]

According to Andrew Brod, an economic analyst in Kernersville, North Carolina (where Hooker closed a plant formerly employing hundreds), many American companies, rather than making capital investments in the U.S., have decided to "funnel investments abroad, many to China itself...." "Some have contracted with Chinese producers, but others have entered into joint ventures to establish new factories [and] to refurbish existing factories," Brod observed.[17]

The closing of the Kernersville Hooker plant had immediate local economic impact. "If I don't work, I can't go out and spend money to shop or buy what I need, so that's going to put somebody else in jeopardy," former Hooker employee Mildred Stiles pointed out. Rather than being "that trickle-down thing," she continued, "I think it's going to be more of a pour-down.... I think it's going to hurt everybody concerned."[18]

In some economic circles, the phenomenon she describes

is called the "race to the bottom" — the sudden precipitous decline of an entire population from the middle class to near-subsistence living.

Our nation's manufacturing sector has been the gateway to the middle class for untold millions of Americans, resulting in unprecedented national prosperity. What will America look like if manufacturing jobs continue to be "outsourced" to low-wage foreign competitors? Surveying Kernersville's grim economic prospects, Brod declares: "In part, the answer to that question is, 'What sort of America do you see now?' It's here already."[19]

De-industrializing the U.S.

"We're killing ourselves," laments Jerry Skoff, owner of a Wisconsin manufacturing firm and member of Save Our American Manufacturing (SAM). "Bombs are falling, but people aren't paying attention. We're being reduced from a manufacturing and hi-tech economy into a service economy — and if things continue the way they are, the service sector will eventually go the same direction."[20]

As noted in the previously cited *Wall Street Journal* story, once manufacturing jobs are "outsourced" to low-wage countries, they almost certainly won't be coming back. Furthermore, the process of exporting industrial jobs necessarily entails de-industrializing the U.S. — and this cycle can become self-sustaining.

"Once tooling capacity is lost, manufacturing simply has to move," observes John C. McCoy, owner of Omnitech Technical Associates in Washington State. "People running companies in this country generally don't want to go offshore. But once the process got started, it snowballed, because the specialized tooling capacity started to shut down — and it takes a long time to re-tool, too long to remain competitive in this globalized economy."

As the U.S. loses its manufacturing capacity, continued Mc-

Coy, "China is being set up as the center of global manufacturing. They have a huge supply of cheap labor, cheap power, and very modern production facilities. Many, perhaps even most, of the Chinese-made products being unloaded on our docks and reaching our store shelves are assembled in automated plants, and dropped into shipping boxes without ever being touched by human hands." Many of those ultra-modern Chinese plants have been built by Japanese firms, but others have been built in recent years by U.S.-based multinational corporations.[21]

China's state-controlled economy rests on a foundation of low-wage and outright slave labor. This offers radical advantages to Chinese firms in their competition with U.S. manufacturers. It also provides the regime with a gusher of revenue it can use to subsidize key industries — in some instances, destroying American competition.

Jay Bender, owner of Falcon Plastics in Brookings, South Dakota, has described how a key customer — a manufacturer of fishing lures — moved its production base from the U.S. to China. Prior to making the move, the customer asked Bender to make a bid on molds used to make the lures. Bender bid $25,000 per mold; the Chinese counter-offer was $3,000 apiece. "I can't even buy raw materials for that," Bender protested. "There are two possibilities: Either they are subsidized by the government, or they gave away the molds to get the manufacturing business." In order to remain in business, Bender had to lay off nearly one-third of his workforce.[22]

There's also a severe price to be paid for relocating manufacturing to China, however.

"Every firm that sets up for production in China has to turn over its technology," notes Jerry Skoff. "Intellectual property theft by the Chinese is very common. And any investment banker familiar with the Chinese system will tell people preparing to set up over there that they should pad their expenses by at least forty percent to allow for the graft, bribes, and other payoffs involved in doing business over there."[23] Nonetheless, U.S. firms continue to "outsource" their manufacturing to China.

A multi-institutional academic study compiled in 2001 reported: "In the months since the enactment of Permanent Normal Trade Relations (PNTR) legislation with China there has been an escalation of production shifts out of the U.S. and into China.... [B]etween October 1, 2000 and April 30, 2001 more than eighty corporations announced their intentions to shift production to China...." According to the study, "as many as 760,000 U.S. jobs have been lost due to the U.S.-China trade deficit since 1992," with a comparable number of jobs disappearing as the result of "outsourcing" to Mexico. "The employment effects of these production shifts go well beyond the individual workers whose jobs were lost," continues the report. "Each time another company shuts down operations and moves work to China, Mexico, or any other country, it has a ripple effect on the wages of every other worker in that industry" — in other words, accelerating the "race to the bottom."[24]

Strategic Vulnerability
Building Beijing's industrial capacity at U.S. expense obviously poses other serious problems — not the least of which is the strategic threat to the U.S. posed by the Communist behemoth. The case of Magnequench, an electronics firm in Valparaiso, Indiana, illustrates the interconnected economic and strategic aspects of "outsourcing" to China.

In 1995, Magnequench was bought by a business consortium including Chinese interests. A few years later, the consortium announced its intention to relocate the plant to China — a move that would deprive the small community of 225 well-paying manufacturing jobs. Just as importantly, it would provide Beijing with a key military technology: Magnequench makes 80 percent of the rare earth magnets used in American "smart bomb" technology.[25]

As the Magnequench example illustrates, the erosion of the U.S. industrial base "has enormous national security implications," observed *National Defense* magazine. "It has made the United States so dependent on foreign countries for critical components and systems that it may have lost its ability to control its supply chains. The United States is becoming dependent on countries such as China, India, Russia, France and Germany for critical weapons technology. It's conceivable that one of these governments could tell its local suppliers not to sell critical components to the United States because they do not agree with U.S. foreign policy."[26]

Business analyst Barry Lynn points out that many of America's premier corporations — including key defense-related firms — now consider themselves to be "virtual companies" depending on a complex and widely dispersed network of suppliers around the world. Dell Computer, for example, assembles its computers out of 4,500 parts manufactured in various Asian countries, including Communist China. Dell — an important defense contractor — maintains an inventory sufficient for only four days' production. If its supply line were interrupted for more than 96 hours, Dell's Texas plants would cease production.[27]

Simply put, "the U.S. industrial base is being taken apart, piece-by-piece, and relocated to other nations," conclude trade analysts Pat Choate and Edward Miller. "In the process, much of America's industrial and military production base is being sold to foreign interests, and more importantly a significant portion of it is being physically relocated into other nations, including our most likely strategic rival — China."[28]

For more than a century and a half, America's manufacturing economy attracted hard-working people from around the world who were eager to become Americans. Manufacturing jobs not only enabled these new arrivals to get on the ladder to the middle class, but helped them to assimilate into our nation's civic culture. But as former Treasury Department official Paul Craig Roberts points out, "The loss of high productivity jobs takes away the ladders of upward mobility and wipes out human capital."

As our manufacturing base is being stripped away, Americans may someday find it necessary to *emigrate* in order to find manufacturing jobs.

No Americans Need Apply

It's a short step from outsourcing manufacturing jobs to China, to outsourcing American workers there. And it's not just factory workers who may someday have to take such drastic steps to preserve their livelihoods. Americans in hi-tech, "information age" positions are seeing their jobs disappear as well.

Daniel Soong graduated from Sacramento State University in 1995 with a degree in computer science. An avid "computer geek" from the earliest age, Soong entered the job market at the peak of the info-tech boom. Fresh out of college he got a position with computer chip maker Intel. Two years later he snagged his "dream job" as a traveling consultant for Boston-based PriceWaterhouseCoopers. In 1999 he went back to California to work for a "dot-com" start-up, but the venture quickly folded. But this didn't discourage Soong: "My skills were in demand." He eventually landed a position with Accenture, an East Coast investment firm.

And then the "outsourcing" began.

"I was in a building with 500 people," recalls Soong. "Then they started to offshore. Nine months later we were down to 50 people." Desperate to find a stable job, Soong seemingly found one with ChevronTexaco, working on a project in San Ramon, California. Hoping that his six-month contract would grow into a full-time position, Soong noticed something disturbing: The project employed a large — a growing — number of foreign workers in the U.S. on H-1B and L-1 visas.

Rather than training American employees, Soong and his

fellow consultants were training guest workers and offshore personnel. And through a slow, steady, but subtle process of attrition, the Americans were being let go. At the end of each two-week pay period, a score or so of the American workers would receive their pink slips.

In January 2003, Soong — halfway through his six-month, $60,000 contract — was called into a meeting with two senior corporate personnel, and sternly told that his performance was inadequate. "I told them my program works great, I had trained everyone, and my full-time ChevronTexaco manager can back me up," Soong relates. "The room was silent for a minute.... Then they just came up with another excuse."

Like so many others in the tech field — engineers, programmers, software designers — Soong found that his job had been outsourced — and that the company had used him to train his foreign replacements. The most tragic case of this sort involved Kevin Flanagan, a programmer for Bank of America (and former Chevron employee) who shot himself to death in May 2003 after being forced to train his replacement employee from India.[29]

"Soong began looking for work, but he soon realized the job market had changed," related *CIO Magazine*. "No one he knew could find a job." Referred to a position in Texas, Soong arranged a telephone interview, only to be hung up on "after 15 seconds." His friends informed him that the company "only interviewed Americans to be in compliance with the equal opportunity employment commission, and that no Americans were ever hired."[30]

By taking piecework (usually for $10 an hour), Soong was able to pay his bills. He continued to make his daily rounds of employment agencies, and to show up for job interviews, but he became convinced that the interviews were perfunctory gestures made by companies bent on sending the work offshore.

Soong eventually decided to send his resume abroad in hopes of finding work in his field. "It would be really interesting to work in Bangalore [India]," he mused. "But I was told, 'Daniel, it is against the law for you to work here. You can come here on vacation, but you can't work here.' "[31]

Experiences of this sort have become heartbreakingly common across the length and breadth of America's hi-tech sector. William F. Jasper, Senior Editor for *The New American* magazine, described the Dickensian scene that unfolded at the Austin headquarters of Dell Computers just two weeks before Christmas 2002. Hundreds of Dell employees gathered for a "town hall" meeting at the Austin campus, ill prepared for the message that senior vice president Jeff Clarke was about to deliver:

> Meetings of this sort were usually big on awards, recognition, and introductions of new products and project teams. And despite the market drubbing of tech stocks in general, Dell had posted another banner year in sales, growth, and profits. The company also benefitted from a nice cash balance, Mr. Clarke noted. Then came the bad news. The company was announcing new personnel 'attrition goals' of 10 percent per year, about double the normal attrition rate. These positions would not be filled in the United States, Clarke explained. They would be filled by new hires in India, China, and other countries where Dell is shifting business.

"Audible gasps came from the employee audience, a hi-tech assemblage of Dell software engineers, electrical engineers, test engineers, group managers, and administrative talent," continued Jasper's account. "A Dell employee who attended the meeting told *The New American*: 'A definite pall came over the crowd. It did not make for a happy Christmas.' "

There had been portents of such a development at Dell since 2000, when Dell opened its China Design Centre in Communist China. Shortly thereafter began a "steady trickle of Red Chinese engineers, project planners, and managers ... brought to Dell's Austin campus for training, and some U.S. Dell employees [began making] the trek to China for four-to-six-month stints to train Chinese personnel there. Around the Dell headquarters in Austin, employees had begun wryly referring to the 'Chinese invasion' as 'training our replacements.' Few expected that the replacing would start so soon."[32]

"Jobs that stay put are becoming a lot harder to find these days," observed *Time* magazine in mid-2003. "U.S. companies are expected to send 3.3 million jobs overseas in the next 12 years, primarily to India, according to a study by Forrester Research. If you've ever called Dell about a sick PC or American Express about an error on your bill, you have already bumped the tip of this 'offshore outsourcing' iceberg. The friendly voice that answered your questions was probably a customer-service rep in Bangalore or New Delhi. Those relatively low-skilled jobs were the first to go, starting in 1997. But more and more of the jobs that are moving abroad are highly skilled and highly paid — the type that U.S. workers assumed would always remain at home."[33]

"No longer is it just Disney toys and Nike shoes made in Haiti and Indonesia," added the *Christian Science Monitor*. "It's software engineering, accounting, and product development being 'outsourced' to India, the Philippines, Russia, and China."

As with the exodus of manufacturing jobs, the outsourcing of Information Technology jobs may have permanent consequences for our nation's economic and technical standing. Basheer Janjua, who presides over Integnology Corp, a firm specializing in domestic outsourcing, points out that U.S. corporations who outsource IT jobs are training the workforces of our future economic (and, in China's case, strategic) competitors. "What's going to be the incentive for our future generations to get a degree in electrical engineering?" asks Janjua. "We have to ask if we're ready to give up our pioneering position in the world."[34]

The Dream Is Dying

We need to ask some even more elemental questions. If Americans aren't *making* anything, how will they be able to make a living? Is it possible to maintain a middle-class standard of living in a service-based economy? Given that (as we'll examine in a later chapter) our nation is importing a third-world population even as it outsources our jobs, will there soon be any service-economy jobs left for Americans to occupy?

Although Americans are glutted on cheap consumer goods, their standard of living — measured in tangible wealth that can be transmitted to their heirs — has declined precipitously during the last thirty years.

"A short generation ago, the greatest country on the face of the earth realized an impossible dream: America put a man on the moon," wrote political analysts Louis T. March and Bret Nelson. "But not only was the American Dream evident in outer space — right here at home one American worker with a high school diploma could support a family. Anytime in American history before the 1970s, the average worker — farmer, stevedore or salesman, it didn't matter — could support his family better and better with each ensuing generation. Nowadays most people find supporting a family on one income is just about as difficult as going to the moon."

"Educated young people look longer and harder for jobs," continue March and Nelson. "Veteran workers find no security in seniority — or in their pension funds. Multinational corporations increasingly treat their employees like equipment — with minimum maintenance, lower operating costs, built in obsolescence and cheap off-shore replacements.... Nowadays when pink slips appear, retraining and counseling programs are the solution. Those fortunate enough to keep their jobs receive lower, adjusted-for-inflation pay than the previous generation. This has been the trend since 1973 — there is something dreadfully, dreadfully wrong."[35]

The Debt Monster

Looming behind this disheartening trend is a mountainous accumulation of household consumer debt.

"A generation ago, a typical American middle-class family lived on the income of a single breadwinner," noted a *USA Today* front-page story. "In recent years it has taken two working spouses to live the middle-class dream. Now, it seems even that is not enough to survive the skyrocketing cost of housing, health care and college while saving for retirement and shouldering growing debt loads."

Although most middle-income families are burdened with credit-card debt, the typical American family doesn't splurge on designer clothes, exotic travel, gourmet food, or other extravagances. Instead, they "are using credit cards to fill in a gap between their income and their costs," according to financial counselor Tamara Draut. "It's more about maintaining their standard of living than frivolous consumption."[36]

Not surprisingly, the combination of widespread consumer debt and a contracting job market has produced an unprecedented number of bankruptcies. According to the Consumer Bankruptcy Project at Harvard University, approximately one-third of families who file for bankruptcy owed *an entire year's salary* on their credit cards. And while credit card debt declined modestly in 2001, this was achieved mainly by trading high-interest credit card debt for lower-rate home equity loans. But home refinancing — one of the faltering pillars of America's consumer economy — compounds, rather than solves, the problem of household debt by putting homes at risk.[37]

As with credit card debt, home equity loans and second (and third) mortgages are being used by many households to make ends meet. In a study of the "mortgage-refinancing binge" of the early 2000s, Dr. Kurt Richebächer examined "the pattern of consumer spending from 2002's first quarter to 2003's first quarter. What we found greatly surprised us."

Apart from a small and short-lived surge in motor vehicle

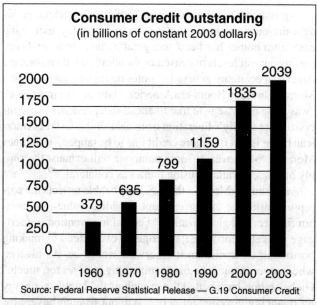

Consumer Credit Outstanding
(in billions of constant 2003 dollars)

Year	Value
1960	379
1970	635
1980	799
1990	1159
2000	1835
2003	2039

Source: Federal Reserve Statistical Release — G.19 Consumer Credit

Rising consumer debt reflects the pressures on our standard of living. A Harvard study revealed that approximately one-third of families who filed for bankruptcy owed *an entire year's salary* on their credit cards.

sales (propelled, to some extent, by zero percent, five-year financing offers), "expenditures on consumer durables were flat over the year," Dr. Richebacher reports. "Among nondurable goods, the major increases in spending were on food, gasoline, and fuel … [and] 64 percent of the higher consumer spending was on services, and mainly on housing and medical care."

This is to say that Americans — many supposedly members of the middle class — were plundering equity from their homes, and assuming enlarged debt burdens, to pay for necessities, not luxuries. "It was a discovery that shocked us — because we learned that the American consumer's heavy borrowing is largely financing expenditures on essentials," summarized Richebacher.[38]

The national economy has been similarly dependent on this debt-driven surge in consumer spending. "Today, extracting cash from homes has become a great hidden slush fund supporting current levels of consumer spending and, therefore, the American economy generally," notes financial analyst Robert Morrow. In Baby Boom-era America, "burning the mortgage" "was a rite of passage to true financial independence"; it symbolized the family's liberation from debt. But now "the American home is just one more credit line to be tapped," continues Morrow. "Moreover, at some point, we will exhaust the supply of money available using homes as collateral."[39]

According to Morrow, the U.S. debt bubble reflects the corrupting influence of "government subsidies, value-free modern finance, and globalization." Federal intervention in mortgage markets "encourage[s] people to overextend by making borrowing cheaper than it otherwise would be. As always, when government subsidizes something, we get too much." Globalization has abetted the growth of the bubble economy by financing government debt: "Without foreign buyers [of debt, both private and government], the wave of cash-out refinancing and home equity loans would reverse, and we would return to the normal mode of gradually paying down mortgages."[40]

Eventually, the bubble will burst. It simply has to. "Homebuyers depend on their jobs to make their mortgage payments, and the economic contraction caused by a squeeze on consumer spending will put those jobs in jeopardy," Morrow warns. And as we've seen, the jobs on which those homes depend are being sent abroad. Thus it's not surprising that as our nation's manufacturing base has shrunk, mortgage delinquencies and foreclosures have accumulated at an unprecedented rate.[41]

At the same time, the federal government is accumulating unprecedented debts — a $600 billion annual deficit, and a national debt approaching seven trillion dollars. What happens if — or, to be perfectly candid, *when* — foreign interests stop lending us money?

"The global money market is a fickle lover," concludes Morrow. "Once money stops blowing into a debt bubble, the bubble bursts, and no financial intervention can restore it. Just ask the Malaysians, the Russians, the Argentineans...."[42]

Since our government owes the national debt in dollars, one likely scenario involves "monetizing" the debt — that is, simply printing up worthless dollars to pay off the debt, which is tantamount to repudiating it — while destroying the purchasing power of American consumers. Christopher Wood of Credit Lyonnais Securities Asia in Hong Kong foresees the impending inflationary collapse of the dollar.

"So long as America continues to secure easy funding, there is no pressure on policymakers in Washington to do anything other than run super-easy policies to try to keep their own consumer credit cycle going," Wood wrote in a 2003 overview of the global economy. "The current trend can continue for a while.... But the longer American excesses are financed, the more inevitable will be the ultimate collapse of the U.S. paper-dollar standard.... The view here is that the US dollar will have disintegrated by the end of this decade."[43]

What Wood describes is hyperinflation — the swiftest way to destroy the middle class. Hyperinflation in the 1920s wiped out the German middle class, clearing the field for the rise of National Socialism. A plausible variation of that doomsday scenario, Morrow suggests, would be "polarization of the American political system between those serving the interests of foreign creditors and those representing American mortgage-holders."[44]

In brief, our current course will lead to abolition of both the middle class and our national independence.

Tragedy — by Design

How did our nation arrive at this pass? Is our decline the result of irrepressible historical forces, or is there a design at work? If the latter is true, who is responsible, and what do they want? And can they be stopped?

The bad news is that America has been led to the brink of disaster by design. The good news is that those responsible for leading our nation to the precipice can be stopped before our nation plunges into Third World status.

During the mid-20th century, Taylor Caldwell was one of the world's best-selling novelists. A careful student of history and current events, Caldwell used her novels to depict, in lightly fictionalized form, the perennial struggle for human freedom and dignity, the chief enemy of which is a deeply entrenched international elite that seeks total power. In order for that elite to rule, Caldwell understood, "the middle class [would have] to be destroyed...."

The following chapters will examine, briefly, the baleful handiwork of that internationalist elite:

- The shackling of American business in socialist regulations, which has driven much of our manufacturing abroad (Chapter Two);
- The rapidly unfolding plot to amalgamate our nation with the other countries of the Western Hemisphere into a socialist regional government akin to the European Union (Chapter Three);
- The creation of a framework for a centrally managed global economy, in which our economic fortunes — both individual and national — would be determined by unelected foreign bureaucrats (Chapter Four);
- Opening our borders to an unrelenting flood of foreign immigrants, both legal and illegal, thereby undermining our national security, national independence, distinctive cultural heritage, and standard of living (Chapter Five);
- The escalating assault on traditional American moral standards and institutions (Appendix I);
- The entanglement of our nation in foreign conflicts, many

of which are explicitly intended to advance the creation of a centralized political system directed by the United Nations (UN), and a centrally directed global economy under the supervision of the World Trade Organization (WTO) (Appendix II).

None of these developments "just happened," and none of the dire consequences that flow therefrom can be considered unavoidable. The closing chapter (Chapter Six) will describe how we can save our nation and create a better world for our children.

But before examining a remedy, we must first survey the damage.

CHAPTER TWO

Banishing Businesses

*The trial has been held. The businessman has been con-
victed. The crime will be announced at a suitable occa-
sion.*

— Ludwig von Mises[1]

*We've lost our steel industry already, and we've vir-
tually lost a big chunk of the automobile industry. And
so now the government is working very, very hard to try
to lose the chemical industry and the paper industry and
the metals industry. I think their energy policy is set up
so that it will drive Americans out of these businesses....
It just breaks my heart. But little by little, we've shifted
and bought and moved businesses to where they are user
friendly.... The government has always been antagonis-
tic toward industrial businesses in America.*

— Chemical magnate Jon M. Huntsman[2]

In 1933, when Adolf Hitler's National Socialist Party came
to power in Germany, the result was what leftist historian
William Shirer called a "Niagara of thousands of special decrees and laws." So vast was the number of those enactments,
and so opaque was the bureaucratic jargon in which they were
written, that "even the most astute businessman was often lost,
and special lawyers had to be employed to enable the firm to
function."[3] German citizens were hard-pressed to learn all of
the laws, let alone obey them.

Although the United States of America is decidedly *not*
Hitler's Reich, Americans — particularly businessmen — are
caught in a remarkably similar regulatory web. If, as the ancient Roman statesman Cicero maintained, free societies are

defined by the existence of a relatively small number of clear, easily understood laws, then the U.S.A. is much closer to Hitler's tyranny than the republican ideal to which our Founders aspired.

"We are a nation of lawbreakers," lamented a *Wall Street Journal* front-page story more than a decade ago. "Nearly all people violate some laws, and many people run afoul of dozens of others without ever being considered, or considering themselves, to be lawbreakers." The result of this proliferation of laws (including bureaucratic enactments that are enforced as if they were laws) is that Americans are left in a state of perpetual insecurity, since "laws that are often broken with impunity make it difficult for people to predict the consequences of their acts."[4]

Each year, literally thousands of new regulations are emitted by the Environmental Protection Agency; the Departments of Transportation, Treasury, Agriculture, Housing and Urban Development, and Interior; the Occupational Safety and Health Administration; and so on. And as the regulatory leviathan grows, it increasingly sucks up revenue, resources, and manpower that otherwise would be invested in productive pursuits — thereby driving an increasing number of businessmen and investors offshore.

Many — perhaps even most — of the U.S. businesses that relocate production offshore are run by people who would prefer to keep the work here at home. Some companies — such as Wisconsin-based engine manufacturer Briggs & Stratton — have actually done battle with the regulatory behemoth in the interest of saving jobs in this country.

In September 2003, Briggs & Stratton Co., which produces small engines (such as those found in lawn mowers and generators), tried to beat back a regulatory assault that would have cost tens of thousands of Americans their jobs. The California State government proposed a new pollution standard requiring small-engine manufacturers to put catalytic converters on their motors beginning in 2020. "We could not do that economically here," protested Briggs & Stratton senior vice president Thomas Savage, warning that re-tooling to meet the standard would probably result in outsourcing the work overseas.[5]

That warning caught the ear of Wisconsin Senator Herbert Kohl. Although a liberal Democrat, Kohl also relies heavily on the support of blue-collar industrial voters in a state whose manufacturing base has been radically eroded over the past decade. Accordingly, Kohl suddenly displayed an unusual (for him) skepticism regarding the value of environmental regulation. "In this economy in which 2.5 million manufacturing jobs have been lost, including 75,000 in Wisconsin, regulations that will force more jobs overseas need additional scrutiny," Kohl declared.[6]

The impact of the envisioned outsourcing by Briggs & Stratton would have been felt in nearly half the states of our union: According to a study released by the company, 22,000 jobs in 24 states would be lost were the new standard to be imposed by California. And the relocation would have an impact far beyond the company's payroll. "California is attempting to impose unreasonable standards that force us to consider moving operations overseas, and this would have a tremendous impact not only on our workers but on our suppliers and customers," company V.P. Thomas Savage explained.[7]

Savage further noted that Briggs is "one of the last remaining U.S. manufacturers of small engines and [we're] doing everything we can to keep good high-tech manufacturing jobs from moving overseas." This included making a counter-proposal to the California Air Resources Board "that would reach a level of emissions reductions comparable to CARB's own proposal, but without the high costs and potential job losses."

Unfortunately, Briggs' attempt at conciliation also included supporting a congressional measure promoting "a uniform national emissions standard set by EPA. A patchwork of state laws would make large-scale engine manufacturing nearly impossible."[8] Rather than solving the company's problem in California, this measure would simply spread the misery nationwide — and set the stage for future regulatory impositions that would drive even more companies to "outsource" the work abroad.

Briggs & Stratton succeeded in getting a U.S. Senate committee to block implementation of the California air quality rule. This prompted the Clear Air Trust — a prominent member of the huge, foundation-funded Establishment environmentalist lobby — to demand that the Securities and Exchange Commission (SEC) investigate the company for supposedly misrepresenting its financial status in an official report.[9]

In a filing with the SEC, Briggs said that it did not believe the proposed California air quality rule "will have a material effect on its financial condition or results of operations...." Senator Dianne Feinstein (D-Calif.), a proponent of the proposed rule, denounced Briggs for its "unsavory" tactics: "They are either not telling the truth [in their SEC filing] ... or they are not telling the truth to the American people, or specifically the Senate."[10]

In fact, Feinstein and her eco-radical allies, in their eagerness to punish Briggs & Stratton for impeding the regulatory juggernaut, were engaged in deliberate misrepresentation: The company didn't stand to lose money *if it relocated the jobs offshore*. At issue was the financial health of the company's American workers, not the company itself.

"Can Briggs & Stratton live with California's proposed regulation? Yes," observed Ernie Blazar, a spokesman for Senator Kit Bond (R-Mo.). "But that would require moving almost 2,000 good-paying jobs from Missouri to other countries...." "We never said that we would lose money, and we never said that in our filing with the SEC," explained Briggs vice president Savage. "What we said ... is this California action would have terrible effects on the employees."[11]

This episode offers a revealing glimpse of the process that has led many American companies to "outsource" their production abroad. Too often, news coverage of such corporate decisions is designed to portray corporate leaders as greedy, unpatriotic opportunists who are clinically indifferent regarding the welfare of their employees. More often than not, however, those decisions are driven by government policies that make it economically impossible for companies to remain in the U.S. Indeed, the Briggs & Stratton episode illustrates that government overregulation of business is the single largest impediment to economic competitiveness.

It's also very instructive to note the reaction provoked by Briggs & Stratton's refusal to play by the accepted script. For fighting on behalf of its employees, the company was threatened with a bogus SEC investigation — a potential corporate death sentence in the post-Enron era. But this is actually fairly typical of the behavior of the federal regulatory leviathan, which often seems to have been given the task of job extermination as its prime directive.

The Regulatory Burden

H. Ross Perot memorably described low wage rates abroad as creating a "giant sucking sound" — the metaphorical sound of industrial jobs being drawn abroad. But while low wage rates "suck" U.S. jobs overseas, the ever-growing quantity of federal regulations pushes them abroad just as vigorously.

The regulatory burden on small businesses (fewer than 500 employees) is particularly staggering: $6,957 per employee. In 2003, thousands of new state laws — many of them intended to carry out federal mandates — went into effect, 1,000 of them in California alone.[12] In 1996, the year Congress passed the "Red Tape Reduction Act," the estimated cost of regulatory compliance for small businesses was $700 billion annually.[13]

By 2003 — seven years after this small business "relief"

package was passed amid great fanfare — that figure had risen to $860 billion, or eight percent of our gross domestic product. The *Federal Register*, which compiles the regulations issued every single day by federal regulatory agencies, expanded to 75,606 pages; compare that total with 9,562 pages in 1950, 20,036 in 1970, and 49,795 in 1990.[14] It should be noted that the *Register* is formatted in double-column pages filled with small type, and that each page is generated by executive branch bureaucrats whose pronouncements supposedly have the force of law.

How onerous is this accumulated body of regulations? Consider this: Several U.S. businessmen who have launched enterprises in Communist China reportedly told a financial commentator that "It is so much easier to start a business in China than in the United States, especially in places like Massachusetts and California."[15] And even when aspiring entrepreneurs succeed in starting businesses, the crush of regulation often makes it difficult to run a profit. This is particularly true even if the costs of regulation are passed on to consumers, as they inevitably must be.

Many critics of "outsourcing" insist that the trend is a reflection of corporate greed and pathetic foreign wages. However, as a study compiled by the National Association of Manufacturers (NAM) documents, the federal regulatory burden is the single most important factor behind the exodus of jobs from the U.S.

"U.S. manufacturing has demonstrated the ability to overcome pure wage differentials with trading partners through innovation, capital investment and productivity," comments James Berges, president of Emerson (a St. Louis-based manufacturer of industrial equipment). "But when the additional external costs [of federal regulation] are piled on, the task becomes unmanageable, even in the best companies."[16]

Simply put: Many, or even most, American businessmen who relocate abroad aren't abandoning our nation. They're

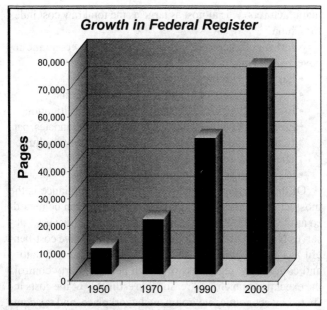

fleeing socialism.

Using a standardized measurement called unit labor costs, the NAM report compares U.S. industrial competitiveness with that of our nine biggest trading partners: Canada, Mexico, Japan, China, Germany, Britain, South Korea, Taiwan, and France. This approach allowed researchers to calculate government-imposed "structural costs" on manufacturing in each country.

According to the report, "domestically imposed costs — by omission or commission of federal, state, and local governments — are damaging manufacturing more than any foreign competitor and adding at least 22.4 percent to the cost of doing business from the United States.... Once these underlying cost pressures are understood, it becomes clearer why much of U.S. production is moving offshore." In fact, the report asserts, "the absolute value of the excess cost burden on U.S.

manufacturers ... is almost as large as the total raw cost index for China."[17]

NAM highlights five "critical obstacles" to economic recovery in the manufacturing sector:

• Excessive corporate taxation.
• Escalating costs of health and pension benefits.
• Escalating costs of actual or threatened tort litigation.
• Escalating compliance costs for regulatory mandates, particularly those related to workplace safety, pollution abatement, and corporate governance.
• Rising energy costs, particularly natural gas.[18]

Of these factors, the cost of regulatory compliance is the most lethal. "Compliance costs for regulations can be regarded as the 'silent killer' of manufacturing competitiveness," observes NAM. "Often developed without an objective cost-benefit analysis, regulations have steadily increased in quantity and complexity, regardless of which political party controls the executive branch." A "reasonable estimate" of the costs inflicted by economic, environmental, workplace, and tax compliance regulations "is in the order of $850 billion — with $160 billion on manufacturers alone, equivalent to a 12 percent excise tax on manufacturing production."[19]

Economist Clyde Wayne Crews Jr. of the CATO Institute points out that "U.S. regulatory costs ... exceed the output of many entire national economies.... U.S. regulatory costs exceed the entire 2000 GDP of Canada, which stood at $701 billion. The regulatory burden also exceeded Mexico's GDP of $574 billion." Estimated federal regulatory costs also exceeded the total of pre-tax corporate profits in 2001 ($699 billion). With U.S. regulatory costs exceeding the GDP of both our "NAFTA partners," and dwarfing total corporate profits, it's not surprising that overburdened American businessmen would be driven abroad in search of more business-friendly environments.

Regulatory costs on small businesses are often referred to

as a "hidden tax" — but this particular tax has a huge and dev-astating ripple effect. As cheaper foreign goods become more available, an increasing number of Americans simply forgo paying the hidden cost of government regulation by choosing less expensive imports. This makes economic sense to con-sumers, at least in the short term. But it also contributes to the outsourcing of production — and jobs — to other countries, which in turn undermines our nation's long-term economic health.

The "Fourth Branch" of Government

The federal regulatory apparatus is often described as the "fourth branch of government." In fact, as economics com-mentator Warren L. McFerran observes, the regulatory agen-cies compose "an entirely separate and independent govern-ment, complete with legislative, executive, and judicial pow-er." Unelected and unaccountable regulators not only devise their own "laws," but are also "empowered to enforce their own rules and act as the accusers against violators [and] function as judge and jury in cases involving their own rules."[20]

As the foregoing cost estimates illustrate, the "fourth branch" also imposes taxes. Economist Crews refers to regu-lation as "off-budget taxation," one of three methods used by the federal government to pay the costs of its programs. The first two, obviously, are direct taxation and borrowing (which contributes to inflation, which is a particularly insidious form of indirect taxation). Through regulation, "rather than pay[ing] directly and book[ing] the expense of a new initiative, [gov-ernment] can require that the private sector and lower-level governments pay.... That process sometimes allows Congress to escape accountability and to blame agencies for costs."[21]

This process has also produced a shadow government with-in our nation that combines legislative, executive, and judicial power. James Madison, in *The Federalist Papers* (essay 47), warned that combining those functions in the same hands "may justly be pronounced the very definition of tyranny." To this indictment of the "fourth branch" must be added the recognition that this illegitimate, unaccountable "shadow government" exercises taxing powers at least equal to that of the legitimate national government.

Another factor driving businesses abroad is our nation's out-of-control system of tort litigation. In 2001, the costs of the U.S. tort system climbed to $205 billion, "or just over 2 percent of GDP," comments the NAM report. "At least one-third of this increase has been due to an upward reassessment of liabilities associated with asbestos claims."[22] Asbestos litigation was an outgrowth of the 1986 Hazard Emergency Response Act, signed into law by President Ronald Reagan, requiring the removal of asbestos in public school buildings. Three years later the Environmental Protection Agency issued regulations effectively banning most uses of asbestos in both public and private buildings by 1997.

Granted, asbestos does pose a public health risk, albeit a relatively moderate one: Constant exposure to significant levels of inhalable asbestos dust can contribute to grave respiratory ailments, including cancer. Those risks were dramatically *increased* by federal policies mandating the removal of asbestos, which disbursed large quantities of asbestos into the air at each affected site. Notes analyst Michael Fumento, "the risk of disease from asbestos in buildings is close to zero."[24] However, a manufactured frenzy that exaggerated the risks of asbestos led to an immensely expensive and utterly counterproductive national drive to remove it from buildings — a campaign that also whetted the destructive appetite of the tort litigation industry.

The economic damage inflicted by the eco-leviathan is hardly limited to asbestos abatement. NAM points out that "pollution abatement falls disproportionately on the shoulders of manufacturers," who accounted for 83 percent of pollution abatement expenditures in 1999. "On a trade-weighted basis," observes the report, "the burden of pollution abatement expenditures alone reduces U.S. cost competitiveness by at least 3.5 percentage points." Of our nine largest economic competitors, only South Korea spends more on pollution abatement as a percentage of GDP; this is true even of the so-called "green" economies of the European Union.[24]

Congressional Abdication

Regulation is a particularly insidious and destructive form of taxation. And it is almost always imposed by faceless, unaccountable bureaucrats, rather than being passed by congressmen who must face the voters and pay the political price of their decisions. As economist Crews points out, "Whatever measures Congress uses to address the regulatory state, dealing with the root of the problem requires ending excessive delegation, or 'regulation without representation.' Congress should not have bureaucrats to blame for regulatory excess that is Congress's fault."[25]

During the late 1990s proposals were made to require Congress "to OK significant agency rules via an expedited process before they are binding," Crews continues. "Article 1 of the Constitution grants legislative power solely to Congress. In that vein, major agency regulations should be turned into bills requiring congressional passage and a presidential signature — no more or less than ordinary legislation. Sensible regulatory policy, as well as constitutional government, demands that every elected representative be on record for significantly costly regulations. Some might complain that voting on regulations would bog down Congress. But do we want Washington making so many laws that lawmakers can't even pass them all during their waking hours?"[26]

Actually, having Congress get bogged down in the process of enacting new regulations would be a very desirable outcome: The longer Congress takes to pass such bills, the likelier that they will wither and die before becoming laws; fewer laws means a reduction in the "hidden tax" that is suffocating our business economy and steadily undermining our standard of living. And as Congress actually assumes the burden it has unconstitutionally delegated to unaccountable bureaucrats, politicians will start absorbing the political costs of regulating productive citizens — which should mean radical reductions of the size and expense of the regulatory state.

Unfortunately, as we will see, our domestic regulatory economy continues its relentless assault on our national wealth, even as a vast apparatus of international regulation is being constructed behind the façade of "free trade."

CHAPTER THREE

Amalgamating the Americas

Eventually our long-range objective is to establish with the United States, but also with Canada, our other regional partner, an ensemble of connections and institutions similar to those created by the European Union.
— Mexican President Vicente Fox, in a 2002 address to the Club XXI in Madrid's "Hotel Eurobuilding"[1]

We cannot leap into world government in one quick step.... [T]he precondition for eventual globalization — genuine globalization — is progressive regionalization, because thereby we move to larger, more stable, more cooperative units.
— Zbigniew Brzezinski, former National Security Adviser and co-founder of the Trilateral Commission, September 28, 1995[2]

"We are determined to consolidate and advance closer bonds of cooperation.... We reiterate our firm adherence to the principles of international law and the purposes and principles enshrined in the United Nations Charter...."
— From the "Declaration of Principles" of the 1994 Summit of the Americas in Miami (the genesis of the Free Trade Area of the Americas)

"We're working to build a Free Trade Area of the Americas [FTAA], and we're determined to complete those negotiations by January of 2005," President George W. Bush told representatives of the Organization for American States (OAS) and the World Affairs Council in Washington,

D.C. on January 16, 2003. The FTAA, continued Mr. Bush, would "make our hemisphere the largest free-trade area in the world, encompassing 34 countries and 800 million people."

At first glance, this seems like an unbeatable win-win proposition: What reasonable person would object to expanding the benefits of "free trade" across the Western Hemisphere? The proposed FTAA quickly earned the exuberant approval from both Republicans and moderate Democrats. Establishment conservatives insisted that the FTAA would be an unalloyed triumph for the free market; many Democrats echoed these assurances as well.

But this assessment fails to account for the Bush administration's apparently contradictory endorsement of international socialism. "The United States' funding for international basic education assistance programs this year will be over 45 percent higher than last year," boasted the president in the same World Affairs Council address. "And this spring, the first of our regional teacher training centers will open in Jamaica. Additional centers will be operating in South and Central America by year's end."

Mr. Bush also noted that his budget for FY 2004 would include a "nearly $50 million increase in aid to the World Bank programs that assist the poorest countries. If the Bank demonstrates it can use the funds to achieve measurable results and helps move forward reform, I'm prepared to consider requesting increases over $100 million in each of my subsequent budgets. This would mean that the amount — the annual U.S. contribution to these World Bank programs — would be 30 percent higher than three years ago."

Hold on a minute: How can "free trade" coexist with expanded international welfare? If the poorer nations of this hemisphere stand to benefit from free trade, why would such welfare be necessary? And what about American taxpayers, whose wealth must be plundered in order to subsidize these international welfare initiatives?

Foreign aid has been aptly described as government theft from poor people in rich countries, to benefit rich people in poor countries. Foreign aid is also a form of bribery — the buying up of political elites in recipient nations. By coupling the "free trade" agenda with promises of expanded foreign aid, President Bush — acting on behalf of those behind the scenes who crafted the proposed FTAA — offered a telling signal as to the real agenda here: "Free trade," as embodied in the FTAA, is not about helping U.S. citizens, or residents of any other nation in this hemisphere; rather, it's intended to serve the interests of the political class.

Free trade is an exchange of goods and services between two parties, unhampered by government intervention. Those involved in such transactions may be neighbors, citizens of the same country, or citizens of different countries. And in order for this exchange to occur, the benefits to each party must outweigh the costs — or else the transaction won't take place.

Another significant benefit to genuine free trade is that it minimizes the role played by government — that is, coercion — in society. When producers and consumers deal with each other in an honorable and mutually beneficial fashion, government's role is merely that of ensuring that neither party defrauds the other. In this way society is shaped by free choices made by individuals, rather than by the heavy-handed intervention of those who want to mold it, by force, in a fashion they deem appropriate.

Simply put, free trade cannot co-exist with large, interventionist government — and the reverse of that statement is true as well. If the burden of regulation and taxation grows too onerous, one result will be the flight of capital abroad to less oppressive business environments. (Ironically, as we saw in the previous chapter, this is true of many American businesses setting up shop abroad: The burdens imposed by our government on business are actually larger and heavier than those inflicted — for now, at least — in Communist China and other countries.) One international benefit of genuine free trade is its ability to undermine oppressive regimes, because — once again — such trade reduces coercion and expands personal choice.

"Upward Harmonization" of Government Power

All of this being said, how does the so-called North American Free Trade Agreement (NAFTA), the precursor to the FTAA, qualify as a "free trade" pact? To accomplish NAFTA's stated intention, a very brief document — perhaps no longer than a few pages — would be necessary. Yet the text of the basic NAFTA is spread across hundreds of pages and divided into two thick, heavy volumes. Much of the language contained therein establishes the foundation for a large, cumbersome international regulatory bureaucracy. Furthermore, at several places the agreement anticipates the creation of additional "annexes" that would create even more layers of international bureaucracy.

NAFTA's implementing legislation also included a provision creating the North American Development Bank (NADBank), a financial institution modeled on the UN-aligned World Bank. Another side agreement to NAFTA created the North American Financial Group (NAFG), which was intended to "stabilize" exchange rates among the three signatory countries. In practice, predictably, both NADBank and the NAFG have served as slush funds or piggy banks for politically protected interests, particularly in Mexico.

Rather than relieving the burden of regulation that impedes genuine free trade, NAFTA internationalized the regulatory apparatus — thereby making it less accountable to the U.S. citizens affected by those regulatory decisions. It is also intended to escalate, rather than reduce, the regulatory assault on commerce.

This last fact was candidly admitted by former U.S. Trade Representative Mickey Kantor as negotiations over NAFTA side agreements ended in August 1993: "No nation can lower labor or environmental standards, only raise them, and all states and provinces can enact even more stringent measures...." [3] The process described by Kantor is called "upward harmonization"; it is the creation of a socialist multi-national government on the installment plan.

Although they are remote from, and not accountable to, the people of the United States, NAFTA's regulatory bodies are very responsive to pressures applied by non-governmental organizations (NGOs). Chiefly composed of foundation-funded labor, environmental, human rights, and sundry radical "activists," the NGO network is often referred to as "international civil society." Their role is to supply "pressure from below" in support of initiatives handed down by the Power Elite, thereby providing an illusion of a broad "consensus." [4] In the case of NAFTA and similar "free trade" agreements, the role played by NGOs is to demand "upward harmonization" of international regulations — even as the NGOs pose as opponents of the trade pacts.

The Center for Science in the Public Interest (CSPI), one of numerous activist groups headed by veteran leftist Ralph Nader, offers a good example of this process at work. For decades, Nader, acting in the role of self-appointed "consumer advocate," has agitated and litigated in pursuit of expanded regulation of the economy. He has done as much as any other private figure to create the massive regulatory burden that is driving businesses offshore. Now Nader and his comrades are using "free trade" pacts as a way of globalizing the same prosperity-killing regulatory burdens.

The October 1999 Congressional testimony of CSPI attorney Benjamin Cohen illustrates how this process works. "Let me state at the outset that we support expansion of international trade.... We also recognize that international harmonization of food safety standards facilitates trade.... The international harmonization process will only benefit consumers if national regulatory standards are harmonized in an upward manner that provides the public with the greatest degree of protection from unsafe foods and deceptive trade practices."[5]

Cohen and his comrades are engaging in a deceptive trade practice of their own — the classic "bait-and-switch." But they're hardly alone in peddling international socialism disguised as free trade.

Consider as well the case of the North American Commission for Environmental Cooperation (NACEC), an advisory body growing out of the NAFTA pact with the role of enforcing multinational environmental standards. The minutes of a typical meeting of the commission's Joint Public Advisory Committee recorded the presentation made by a representative of an "environmental NGO." The representative was complaining about "downward harmonization" of international eco-regulations and invoked Article 1114 of the NAFTA treaty to demand international collaboration in raising regulatory standards throughout the region.[6]

NAFTA created literally scores of regulatory bodies, and left the door open for the creation of many more at whim. Prior to the agreement's enactment, trade analyst Thomas R. Eddlem warned:

Adoption of [NAFTA] … and its side agreements … will create a lot of new high-paying jobs. Unfortunately, most of them will be government positions for bureaucrats working in the more than 30 new international government committees, subcommittees, councils, working groups, and subgroups mandated by NAFTA.... NAFTA itself would establish the Free Trade Council — a continental government-in-waiting with enormous discretionary powers — with at least eight permanent committees, six 'working groups,' and five subcommittees and subgroups. NAFTA's side agreement on import surges would add a permanent 'Working Group on

Emergency Actions,' and the side agreements on labor and the environment would create two additional regional law-making bodies, each with its own bureaucracy and advisory committees.[7]

How does the creation of this huge — and growing — regulatory leviathan aid the process of "free trade"? It doesn't, of course. Nor should it be expected to. It is, after all, the creation of the same ruling elite that has imposed enormous tax and regulatory burdens on American producers. With diabolical guile, that elite has enhanced its powers at considerable expense to America's prosperity — while flying the false banner of "free trade."

"Downward Harmonization" of Living Standards

"Upward harmonization" of government power inevitably produces a corresponding phenomenon — "downward harmonization" of living standards, sometimes called the "race to the bottom." As governing elites pool their power across borders, those they rule lose a corresponding amount of freedom and prosperity.

On the tenth anniversary of the NAFTA accord, the *Christian Science Monitor* noted that the agreement, "while opening the doors for U.S. exports and helping Americans get low-cost consumer goods, has also shaken entire industries from textiles to cars."[8] As our economy has been merged with socialist Canada and corrupt, cartelized Mexico, "NAFTA has displaced American workers and devastated entire towns.... It's evident from the job-training centers in southern Texas to the 'NAFTA ghost towns' of North Carolina, with their shuttered textile plants."[9]

Economist Jorge Gonzalez of San Antonio's Trinity University claims that NAFTA has done "exactly what it is supposed to do.... We've basically taken two economies with vastly different resources [those of the U.S. and Mexico] and in-

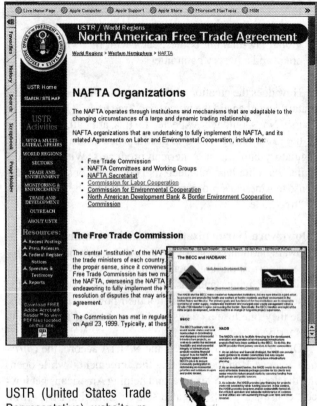

USTR (United States Trade Representative) website reveals the bureaucratic make-up of NAFTA. The page for the BECC (Border Environment Cooperation Commission) and NADBANK (North America Development Bank) states:

"It is widely understood that the NAFTA laid out specific rules for North American trade. Less widely recognized are the many provisions in the NAFTA that instruct or allow the NAFTA parties to agree to additional trade liberalizing measures...."

tegrated them. That helps the whole region become more competitive."[10] Economist Russell Roberts of George Mason University agrees that the political benefits of integrating North America more than compensate for the hardships NAFTA has inflicted on American workers: "The bottom line is this — NAFTA has caused hardship for some Americans in certain sectors, but it's made for a more stable and integrated Mexican political system — and that's a real good thing for the world."[11]

Scant comfort such glib assessments will provide to Americans whose lucrative manufacturing jobs have fled the country. Breadwinners seeking to provide a decent standard of living for their families, and perhaps even leave an inheritance for their children, have little interest in regional "competitiveness," or in helping Mexico become "stable and integrated." But they are the ones paying the price of the Power Elite's grand designs.

And it's important to recognize that while American workers have endured hardships as a result of NAFTA, the ruling class is prospering as never before. Indeed, the Power Elite benefits directly by inducing "downward harmonization" on the working class. This is illustrated by the existence of the so-called "Trade Adjustment Assistance" program — a $1.3 billion federal welfare program for Americans who lose their jobs as a result of NAFTA and other socialist "free trade" initiatives.[12] Wherever it succeeds in reducing the proud, stubborn middle class to a state of welfare dependency, the political class prospers.

Building World Government, Bloc by Bloc

As we can clearly see, the expression "free trade" has been hijacked, tortured, and forced to serve purposes alien to its meaning. In this case, the banner of "free trade" has been wrapped deceptively around a mammoth campaign to abolish national sovereignty and build a socialist regional political bloc.

Here's how the deception works. Sovereign powers exercised by our nation, such as the power to protect our borders and Congress's constitutional role in regulating trade policy, are being depicted as impediments to trade. Removing those barriers, the public is told incessantly, will expand trade and thus increase our national prosperity. But the actual trade-off here involves the surrender of our sovereignty, on a piecemeal basis, to international regulatory bodies governing the various trade blocs.

The so-called Free Trade Area of the Americas (FTAA), scheduled for completion in 2005, would expand on the "progress" made under NAFTA. As the FTAA secretariat explains, the FTAA would "unite the economies of the Americas into a single free trade area ... in which barriers to trade and investment will be progressively eliminated." [13]

Once again, it's important to recognize that the "barriers" referred to in the statement above are actually the characteristics of national sovereignty. Removing them accelerates our descent from prosperity and independence into the pit of international socialism — and, eventually, world government. Enactment of NAFTA represented a major step toward that end; this was attested by comments made in support of that agreement by globally minded luminaries.

Former Secretary of State Henry Kissinger, a member of the executive committee of the Trilateral Commission and a longtime power in the Council on Foreign Relations (CFR) — the two most prominent and influential globalist organizations — stated in a 1993 *Los Angeles Times* op-ed column that NAFTA "will represent the most creative step toward a new world order taken by any group of countries since the end of the Cold War.... "NAFTA "is not a conventional trade agreement," he noted, "but the architecture of a new international system." David Rockefeller, former CFR chairman and co-founder of the Trilateral Commission, went so far as to say in the *Wall Street Journal* that he didn't "think that 'criminal' would be too strong a word to describe … rejecting NAFTA." Exhorted Rockefeller: "Everything is in place — after 500 years — to build a true 'new world' in the Western Hemisphere." Andrew Reding of the New School for Social Research, a radical New York think-tank, described NAFTA as "an incipient form of international government," that would "signal the formation, however tentatively, of a new political unit — North America."[14]

NAFTA, like the European Union (EU), is a political subsidiary of the World Trade Organization (WTO). As we will see in the next chapter, the WTO is the economic complement to the United Nations. Professor Nicole Anne Stubbs of the University of Washington observes: "The EU and NAFTA both play by the same set of global trade rules set today by the World Trade Organization.... This represents a common thread between the two regional institutions." The chief difference between these two trade blocs is that "The EU has deepened and widened while adhering to multilateral institutions such as the WTO."[15]

The terms "deepening" and "widening" refer to the EU's territorial expansion and the growth of its socialist regulatory bureaucracy. Significantly, FTAA supporters admit that the proposed agreement represents a "deepening" and "widening" of NAFTA — the creation of an economic and political unit encompassing everything from Alaska to Tierra del Fuego, ruling the entire hemisphere as a subsidiary of the WTO.

The American "Soviet"
As Mexican President Vicente Fox frankly told an audience in Madrid, the objective is to create "an ensemble of connections and institutions similar to those created by the European Union." The EU, significantly, has been described by former Soviet ruler Mikhail Gorbachev as a "new European Soviet" — that is, a socialist entity in which all economic, cultural, social, and political questions will ultimately be decided by the

central government in Brussels.

Residents of the formerly independent nations of Europe are required to surrender their currencies, adopting in their place the euro — the value of which will be set by a European central bank. The laws and administrative policies of EU member-states are similarly set by Brussels. Residents of Great Britain could find themselves arrested for offenses against EU laws, extradited, standing trial in front of foreign courts, and serving their sentences in foreign jails. The powers of local and national political bodies are being eclipsed by Brussels, placing questions of taxation, regulation, and even foreign policy in the hands of the socialist Eurocrats.

Similar conditions will prevail in this hemisphere if the FTAA comes into being, and the process of "widening" and "deepening" ensues. Eventually, Americans would find that they are powerless to affect decisions being made by remote international bureaucracies that affect their lives, livelihoods, and liberties. The value of our currency, the scope of regulatory burdens on our businesses, the amount we pay in taxes — all of these decisions would be made by distant, unaccountable bureaucrats whose job is to administer policies handed down from the WTO and the UN, rather than represent the interests of Americans.

In this fashion — through patient, persistent incrementalism, trading bloc by trading bloc — the architecture of a world government is taking shape around us. Although utopian in design, this campaign has real, tangible costs that are being felt in the loss of American jobs and the decline of our middle class as we are rudely and pitilessly "harmonized" down to the level of the less fortunate residents of this hemisphere.

CHAPTER FOUR

Caught in the WTO Web

I am against GATT [General Agreement on Tariffs and Trade, forerunner to the World Trade Organization] because it is part and parcel of international socialism, one-worldism, and the slow surrender of American sovereignty.... GATT ... calls for a vast complex of multilateral negotiations with many nations in a sort of world super-legislature where we have one vote.... Once wrapped up in this spider web, it will be difficult indeed to recapture any independence of action.

— Former Congressman Samuel B. Pettengill
(D-Ind.), 1948[1]

[T]he "house of world order" will have to be built from the bottom up rather than from the top down.... [A]n end run around national sovereignty, eroding it piece by piece, will accomplish much more than the old-fashioned frontal assault.... [W]e will be seeking new rules in the General Agreement on Tariffs and Trade to cover a whole range of hitherto unregulated non-tariff barriers. These will subject countries to an unprecedented degree of international surveillance over up to now sacrosanct 'domestic' policies, such as farm price supports, subsidies, and government procurement practices that have transnational effects.

— Columbia University Professor (and diplomatic
insider) Richard Gardner (CFR), 1974[2]

In November 2003, the President of the United States received a directive to remove protective tariffs on steel imports. The body issuing that order describes itself as the apex tribunal of the global trading system — the Geneva-based Appellate Body of the World Trade Organization (WTO). The WTO tribunal ruled that Washington had failed to demonstrate — to the tribunal's satisfaction, at least — that the U.S. steel industry was genuinely threatened by a surge of imports of steel and related products.[3]

Emboldened by the WTO's ruling, the European Union "immediately warned President Bush that he must quickly withdraw the 20-month-old tariffs or face retaliation" in the form of "$2.2 billion in duties on U.S. goods." 22 nations that had jointly filed a WTO complaint against the tariffs — initially set at 30 percent, but subsequently reduced — insisted that the Appellate Body's ruling "leaves the United States with no other choice but to terminate its WTO-incompatible [tariff] measures without delay."[4]

Incredibly, the assumption that the United States must comply with an arbitrary ruling handed down by a foreign body was not challenged by the White House. President Bush's press secretary maintained that the protective tariffs on steel "were fully consistent with WTO rules." Republican Senator Charles Grassley, head of the Senate Finance Committee, advised President Bush not to undermine the WTO's supposed authority: "Complying with our WTO obligations is an important sign of American leadership."[5]

This was not the first time that the WTO had ruled against the United States. Nor was it surprising that the body, in which the EU outvotes the U.S. 15 to 1, would hand down a decision favoring European interests. As we will see, from the beginning the WTO — like its predecessor, the abortive International Trade Organization — was designed to put America at a disadvantage vis-à-vis the rest of the world.

What is particularly striking about the tariff dispute is how little it had to do with free trade — which consists of mutually beneficial exchanges between buyers and sellers unimpeded by government. When the U.S. approved creation of the

WTO in 1994, its supporters described the body as a necessary measure to lower tariff barriers worldwide.

Jack Kemp, a former Republican congressman and Secretary of Housing and Urban Development, insisted that Republicans "who use the sovereignty issue to oppose [creation of the WTO] will be accused of failing to pass the largest international tax cut in history...."

But under the WTO regime, nations and multinational trading blocs can enact tariffs — when such measures find favor with the unelected globalist gnomes who occupy the WTO's judicial panels. In the case of the United States, the U.S. Congress — which under the U.S. Constitution has the exclusive power to regulate our trade with foreign nations — surrendered this critical legislative power to a globalist body composed of foreign bureaucrats with no interest in our nation's prosperity or sovereignty.

Furthermore, where Republican globalists like Jack Kemp urged Congress to surrender sovereignty in the interest of a tax cut, the actual result was an American defeat on both accounts: Congress surrendered the power to regulate our nation's foreign trade and handed to a globalist body the power to set tax policy. After all, tariffs are taxes — albeit of a much less invasive variety than the income tax. During the administration of Thomas Jefferson, the federal government's revenue came exclusively from the tariff. In his second Inaugural Address, President Jefferson boasted:

> The suppression of unnecessary offices ... enabled us to discontinue our internal taxes.... The remaining revenue on the consumption of foreign articles is paid chiefly by those who can afford to add foreign luxuries to domestic comforts, being collected on our seaboard and frontiers only, and, incorporated with the transactions of our mercantile citizens, it may be the pleasure and pride of an American to ask, "What farmer, what

mechanic, what laborer ever sees a taxgatherer of the United States?"[6]

It is hardly an exaggeration to say that defending American interests in international trade was one of the most important motives for creating a constitutional union out of the thirteen original colonies. And, of course, most Americans — even those only dimly aware of our heritage — recall the emphatic Revolutionary War slogan: "No taxation without representation!" Yet Congress turned over vital powers over our policies on trade and taxes to a cabal of unelected, unaccountable foreign social engineers — and it did so knowingly.

Newt's Coup

The November 1994 mid-term elections resulted in a Republican majority for the first time since the early 1950s. Many — if not most — of the freshman representatives had been propelled into Congress on the strength of the public's concerns over the growing expense and intrusiveness of government, as well as the accelerating loss of American sovereignty to international organizations such as the UN.

Following the election, incoming Senate Majority Leader Bob Dole and prospective Speaker of the House Newt Gingrich agreed to an extraordinary "lame duck" session of the outgoing Congress. The purpose of that session was to approve U.S. membership in the WTO. Given the significance of that issue, why couldn't it await consideration by the incoming Congress, which was more clearly attuned to the public's concerns? And why would two "conservative" leaders be so determined to have this important issue determined by a Democrat-majority Congress?

These questions effectively answer themselves. It was precisely because the incoming conservative Congress — like the public at large — was hostile to entangling commitments such as the proposed WTO that the "lame duck"

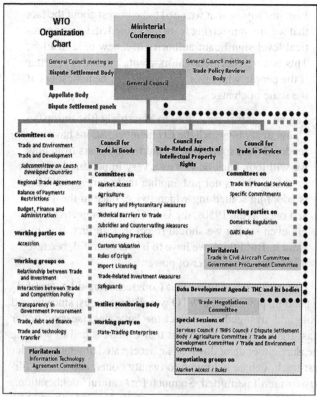

The World Trade Organization (WTO) comprises a vast apparatus to oversee and regulate virtually all aspects of every member nation's trade in goods *and even services.*

session was necessary.

In fact, Gingrich admitted in testimony before the House Ways and Means Committee that congressional approval of the WTO would represent a fundamental change in our economic and political systems by surrendering sovereignty to an emerging world government:

I am just saying that we need to be honest about the fact that we are transferring from the United States at a practical level significant authority to a new organization. This is a transformational moment. I would feel better if the people who favor this would just be honest about the scale of change....

I agree ... this is very close to Maastricht [the European Union treaty by which the EU member nations have surrendered their sovereignty], and twenty years from now we will look back on this as a very important defining moment. This is not just another trade agreement. This is adopting something which twice, once in the 1940s and once in the 1950s, the U.S. Congress rejected. I am not even saying we should reject it; I, in fact, lean toward it. But I think we have to be very careful, because it is a very big transfer of power.[7]

Gingrich's admonition that Congress should be "careful" in handing power to the WTO was disingenuous, since he and Dole had arranged to conduct the lame duck session under "fast-track" rules. This meant that Congress had to vote the measure either up or down on an accelerated timetable: Under fast-track, debate is limited to twenty hours, and Senate filibusters aren't permitted. So much for "careful" deliberation.

Furthermore, as was the case with NAFTA, the GATT agreement creating the WTO was actually a treaty disguised as a trade agreement. By packaging the pact in this fashion, WTO proponents avoided the constitutional requirement that treaties win approval by a two-thirds super-majority in the Senate.

In the WTO, nations of the so-called "Global South" — formerly known as the "Third World," sometimes called, with undue optimism, the "developing world" — possess 70 percent of the votes, and the U.S. has no veto power.

But in addition to surrendering congressional powers, the

WTO, in the words of liberal Harvard law professor Lawrence Tribe, "shifts ... sovereignty from state and local governments" to the global body. This not only gives foreign bureaucrats the power to nullify state and local laws, but also creates new opportunities for a U.S. president to retaliate against political rivals. Shortly before Congress approved the WTO, former Treasury Department official Paul Craig Roberts expressed amazement that "anyone in Congress wants to pass a bill that gives the President sole power to negotiate remedies when the WTO declares federal, state and local laws illegal under GATT. This power gives the White House a free hand to reward friends and to punish enemies."[8]

At first glance this enhancement of presidential power seems to contradict the internationalist thrust of the WTO: Why would the measure empower both a cadre of unelected foreign bureaucrats *and* the U.S. president? Wouldn't the president be inclined to work on behalf of our national interests?

Of course, Americans would expect this of their presidents. In practice, however, every president since Franklin D. Roosevelt has been surrounded by internationalist advisers and has accordingly used the presidential powers to advance globalist designs.

From the internationalist perspective, the role of the executive — whether president, prime minister, or by any other title — is to carry out his nation's "international obligations."

Executive Branch Betrayal

More than four decades ago, George W. Malone, a Republican Senator from Nevada, warned that "a pincers movement is now in operation both on the domestic and on the international scene, and ... evidence shows that this movement bodes no good for us."[9] One jaw of the pincers was political, involving the steady entanglement of our nation in international alliances and multilateral bodies such as the UN.

It's worth noting that Senator Malone, a WWI veteran and

military intelligence specialist, attended the UN's founding conference in San Francisco as an official observer for the Senate Military Affairs Committee. He also toured — at his own expense — Europe, Asia, and the Middle East, primarily to investigate the uses to which U.S. foreign aid was put.[10] A man of substantial academic achievement and considerable firsthand experience, Senator Malone could speak with authority about the developments he described — and their implications for our nation's future.

Through a series of crucial decisions stealthily undertaken by what Malone called a "combination" within our government, "a basic segment of the sovereign power of the people of the United States [was] removed from them and absorbed into the American executive." That power was then used to make a series of commitments in the name of our nation — "the UNRRA [United Nations Relief and Relocation Agency]; Dumbarton Oaks [the secretive meeting to draft the UN Charter]; the Bretton Woods Conference which resulted in the International Bank and Fund; the Preparatory Conference for UNESCO [the United Nations Educational, Scientific and Cultural Committee]; the San Francisco Conference which set up the United Nations; the NATO and SEATO military alliances; the Genocide Convention; the Declaration of Human Rights...."

The result of these decisions, concluded Senator Malone, was that "our people have since been subjected to court interpretations which rest on 'the purposes and principles of the Charter of the United Nations.'"[11]

Once again, that is the "political" jaw of the pincers described by Senator Malone. The "economic" jaw was created by the Trade Agreements Act of 1934, in which Congress yielded to the president the power to control our nation's trade policy — thus allowing the executive branch to surrender that authority to foreign bureaucrats: "That power is now being increasingly vested in international groups, and removed from our Nation's control."[12] The most important of those groups, according to Senator Malone, was the GATT, which he identified as "an instrument of the growing International State."[13]

Building the Socialist World State

Malone warned that the ultimate purpose of the pincers movement was to create a "Socialist World State" in which our nation would lose its independence — and Americans would lose their prosperity and liberty.[14] This was the true purpose of the movement misleadingly labeled "free world trade."

Although that slogan promised freedom from state interference in commerce, what it meant in practice was that "the State would determine trade" — each central government for individual nations, and ultimately a central global trade authority for the entire world.[15] With passage of the Trade Act of 1934, argued Senator Malone, "the business and the enterprise of individuals now were considered in close connection to the policies of the state. The state would assist them in the expansion of their markets. Government would negotiate the channels of trade...."[16]

Roughly a decade later, as war-weary nations were beguiled into supporting a global "peacekeeping" body called the United Nations, the world organization's architects proposed the creation of three economic bodies to supplement the UN: The International Trade Organization (ITO), the International Monetary Fund and the World Bank. In late 1947, a delegation of U.S. internationalists attended a conference in Havana to finish the framework for the ITO.

The Executive Committee Chairman of the *U.S.* delegation to the Havana Conference was the notorious Soviet agent and traitor Alger Hiss.[17] Along with Soviet official V.M. Molotov, Hiss had been the chief co-author of the UN Charter; he also served as secretary-general for the UN's founding conference. Hiss, an eager and capable enemy of our country, clearly regarded the ITO as a means of hastening our nation's destruction.

As would be the case with the WTO, the ITO envisioned a one-nation, one-vote scheme that would leave America's trade policy in the hands of foreign rivals. Congressman Bertrand Gearhart (R-Calif.) described the Hiss-led delegation to the Havana Conference as "boatloads of smug diplomats, all-wise economists ... experts, theorists, specialists and whatnots, sailing gaily from our shores to barter away ... the little factory in Wichita, the little shop in Keokuk." [18]

Fortunately, the ITO collided with the same patriotic opposition that had scuttled the attempt to entangle the U.S. in the League of Nations after World War I.

The final ITO draft was finished on March 24, 1948. But the pact's globalist and socialist provisions provoked opposition from Congress and many of our nation's business associations. The ITO "was described as a charter to 'free world trade,'" recalled Senator Malone. "It was found to be a charter for trade control.... The result of its adoption would have been socialism, on a global plane." [19]

"The entire document reflects an excessive acceptance of economic planning," protested the U.S. Chamber of Commerce. The National Foreign Trade Council warned that "if the United States subscribes to the charter it will be abandoning traditional American principles and espousing, instead, planned economy and full-scale political control of production, trade, and monetary exchange. The charter does not reflect faith in the principles of free, private, competitive enterprise." [20] Because of widespread opposition to the agreement, the ITO was never submitted to Congress for ratification.

But the internationalist Power Elite is never willing simply to take "no" for an answer, preferring to interpret that response as: "Not yet — but someday soon." Just as they had done when the League of Nations failed, the Power Elite regrouped, changed the name of the defeated global body, and prevailed in the 1994 rematch — with the help of globalists in the Republican Party's leadership ranks.

In *Our Global Neighborhood*, the UN-aligned Commission on Global Governance described the WTO's important role in "global governance" (that is, building world government):

> Particularly important is the establishment of a WTO to provide a stronger and more permanent successor to the GATT.... Its establishment will be *a crucial building block for global economic governance*.... The WTO and advanced regional groups such as the EU will increasingly be faced with the issue that will dominate the international economic agenda in years to come: how to create rules for deep integration that go way beyond what has traditionally been thought of as "trade." (Emphasis added).[21]

Strip-mining the U.S. Economy

Just as the GATT — General Agreement on Tariffs and Trade — begat the WTO, GATT and the WTO begat GATS — the General Agreement on Trade in Services. Like other instruments described as "free trade" measures, GATS appears harmless or even beneficial. Just as NAFTA and the WTO are advertised as ways to open up global commerce in goods, GATS is described as a means of opening up global trade in services.

The cold reality, however, is that GATS is another stealthy assault on our national sovereignty and federal system. Through GATS, the WTO is slowly, quietly, but persistently subverting the powers of our state and local governments and bringing literally every service job in the nation under the world trade body's regulatory control.

As the Office of the U.S. Trade Representative points out, "Services are what most Americans do for a living. Service industries account for nearly 80 percent of U.S. employment and GDP [Gross Domestic Product]."[22] With the accelerating exodus of manufacturing and hi-tech jobs from the United States, an increasing number of Americans will find themselves seeking work in service industries. Thanks to GATS, these Americans will find themselves facing the same "race to the bottom" that has claimed so many manufacturing jobs.

GATS is not a single agreement, like NAFTA, or even a standing regulatory body, like the WTO. It is an open-ended process in which hordes of foreign bureaucrats review state and local laws governing the licensing and certification of service workers — from beauticians to attorneys — and any other laws seen as impeding global free trade in services. Through that process, all state and local laws are thrown open to challenge by foreign governments.

Under our constitutional system, all powers not explicitly granted to the central government are reserved to the states and the people. These "numerous and indefinite" powers, to use James Madison's phrase, include the power to establish licensing guidelines for service industries, as well as regulations governing land use and ownership.

It's true, of course, that these powers can be abused by local and state governments. But one assumption behind our constitutional system is that local and state governments would be more immediately accountable to the people and that, where those powers are abused, people would have the option of choosing to live elsewhere. The potential cost of losing productive populations would serve as a check on the regulatory ambitions of state governments. (Indeed, something of this sort happened to California during the 1990s, as business owners and taxpayers fled the over-taxed, over-regulated Golden State.) And under our Constitution, no state government can properly meddle in the regulatory affairs of other states — not that there would really be any incentive to do so: When one state imposes unreasonable regulatory burdens on business and industry, other states with more sensible policies benefit economically.

Our federated constitutional government was the natural

complement to a market-based economy, and this combination led to unprecedented prosperity and technological progress. GATS is an effort to destroy America's economic system by forcing all states and local communities to conform to the edicts of a conclave of globalists in Geneva.

Consider, for example, efforts by European Union GATS negotiators to force state governments to remove "discriminatory" laws regulating accounting, auditing, and bookkeeping services. Secret GATS negotiation documents leaked from Europe record EU objections to laws of several states requiring in-state offices and residency requirements. The EU also demanded removal of residency requirements for engineers, insurance workers, and so forth. The EU also demanded removal of state laws requiring "U.S. citizenship and residency for members of the board and incorporators" of service-related businesses.[23]

It's clear that GATS will eventually facilitate foreign challenges to laws governing the licensing of attorneys, medical professionals, and other highly specialized "service" workers. As twenty-eight Democratic congressmen complained in a letter to the U.S. Trade Representative, "the only services exempted [from the GATS process] would be those services 'supplied in the exercise of governmental authority,' defined as 'any service which is supplied neither on a commercial basis, nor in competition with one or more service providers.' These are critical terms that remain undefined and could be interpreted by a dispute panel in a way that renders the exemption meaningless."[24]

It was the states that created our federal government and allocated it limited, revocable powers; after all, until the early 20th century, "United States" was understood to be a plural construction, as in "these united States in Congress assembled...." The process of consolidating the states into a monolith under the power of the central government began with the post-Civil War Reconstruction, gained momentum during

World War I, accelerated radically during the New Deal, and has continued relentlessly ever since. The GATS process represents the next logical step: Putting state governments under the control of a global central government.

Once again, the rationale offered by proponents for this power grab is the necessity of removing impediments to "free trade." Among these "impediments" are the powers reserved to the states for the specific purpose of protecting the people against the encroachments of the central government. The distant, unaccountable bureaucrats seeking to absorb those powers certainly don't have our nation's best interests in mind.

Exporting Jobs, Importing Workers

Through the H-1B and L-1 visa programs, foreign non-immigrant specialty workers are permitted to work in the United States. As noted in Chapter One, these programs have been used to train the workforces of foreign competitors, thereby fueling the outsourcing of technical jobs overseas.

The 1995 GATS agreement locked the United States into an annual ceiling of 65,000 H-1B visas, and an unlimited number of L-1 visas (which permit inter-company transfer of foreign workers from abroad to the U.S.). Just as importantly, it inaugurated a process through which foreign interests can challenge any limits on such temporary immigration as "discriminatory" — thereby forcing our nation to continue building a well-trained workforce that will benefit our economic competitors. Dan Stein of the Federation for American Immigration Reform points out that under GATS, "the United States bound itself by international agreement not to restrict either of these visa programs in the future, regardless of the state of the US economy or the level of unemployment of similarly qualified U.S. workers."[25]

"It is often difficult to tell these days if economies exist to serve the needs of people, or the other way around," continues Stein:

Trade policies that include provisions for unfettered movement of people across international borders for the purpose of providing ever-cheaper labor lead us further down the path toward standing the relationship between people and economics on its head. At some point, the pursuit of cheaper products and cheaper workers becomes a race to the bottom, which in the long run will cripple middle-class American families and destroy access to the American dream for millions of American workers.... Far from improving the quality of life for middle-class Americans, [so-called "free trade" agreements like GATT/WTO and GATS] will eventually destroy the American middle class.[26]

It's important to remember that, free-market rhetoric notwithstanding, the purpose of GATT/WTO, GATS, NAFTA, and similar "free trade" pacts is to consolidate power, not to expand prosperity. The real objective is to destroy national sovereignty and erect a global government, not to remove impediments to honest commerce. Legitimate free trade is the path to reduced government and expanded individual liberty; the globalist counterfeit being offered today is a highway to universal serfdom.

CHAPTER FIVE

Electing a New People

If the government doesn't like the people, why doesn't it dissolve them and elect a new people?
— Marxist playwright Berthold Brecht, 1953

[Illegal immigrants are] a nation within a nation, society within a society, that alone possesses the numerical and positional strength to undermine the American empire from within.... [T]his "nation within a nation" can act to bring "socialism" to North America by virtue of a combined hemispheric process of revolt that overlaps boundaries and interlaces movements.
— Marxist theoretician Mike Davis, in *Prisoners of the American Dream*[1]

A peaceful mass of people ... carries out slowly and patiently an unstoppable invasion, the most important in human history.... [The invasion] seems to be slowly returning [the southwestern United States] to the jurisdiction of Mexico without the firing of a single shot, nor requiring the least diplomatic action, by means of a steady, spontaneous, and uninterrupted occupation.
— Mexican commentator Carlos Loret de Mola, writing in *Excelsior*, 1982[2]

Mexico is a friend of America. Mexico is our neighbor. And we want our neighbors to succeed. We want our neighbors to do well.... And that's why it's so important for us to tear down barriers and walls that might separate Mexico from the United States.
— President George W. Bush, address to the Hispanic

Chamber of Commerce, Albuquerque, New Mexico,
August 15, 2001[3]

President George W. Bush's January 7, 2004 announcement
of an ambitious plan to extend amnesty to millions — or
tens of millions — of illegal immigrants triggered a sudden
rush on our southern border.

"The U.S. Border Patrol marks January 7 as the day illegal
crossing numbers surge," reported an *Arizona Star* dispatch
from Hermosillo, a Mexican border town frequently used as a
jumping-off point for illegal immigration. Mexicans arrive at
the border by foot, bus, and train. Mexicana airlines and three
other Mexican air carriers have thoughtfully arranged special
flights that carry hundreds of border-jumpers to Hermosillo
each day. Once there, those seeking to enter the U.S. illegally
often place themselves in the care of immigrant smugglers,
known as *coyotes*. Hundreds die each year as they try to make
the dangerous desert crossing into Arizona in search of work.[4]

A similar "amnesty rush" ensued across the southwestern
border. At the San Ysidro port of entry — the world's largest
land-based border crossing — Border Patrol officials noted a
sharp increase in the use of fraudulent identification papers in
the immediate aftermath of President Bush's announcement.
More than half of those caught with counterfeit documents admitted that the amnesty offer induced them to attempt to enter
the U.S. illegally.

Not surprisingly, active and former Border Patrol agents
were less than enamored of the Bush amnesty proposal.
"Everybody thinks it's a slap in the face," commented San
Diego-based agent T.J. Bonner, head of the 10,000-member
Border Patrol Council. The council's vice president, John
Frecker, concurred in that view, noting further in a letter to
Border Patrol agents that the amnesty proposal "implies that
the country really wasn't serious about [immigration control]
in the first place, in spite of what you were told about the 'big

picture.' "[5]

Agents of the U.S. Border Patrol carry out a vital and unique role by literally guarding our nation's frontiers against foreign invasion. In the line of duty the men who compose the "Thin Green Line" of the Border Patrol face hardship, danger, and occasionally death at the hands of drug and alien smugglers. Agents are often called on to provide medical care to people cruelly abandoned to their fate by the venal, corrupt *coyotes*.

The Border Patrol's work is difficult and largely thankless even at the best of times. An amnesty for illegal aliens makes that job almost impossible. "In 1986, we had the first amnesty, it was supposed to be a one-shot deal," pointed out retired Border Patrol Agent Mike Cutler. At the time, the illegal alien population was estimated at roughly 3-6 million. By 2004, it had increased to at least 8-12 million.[6]

This reflects the unfortunate reality that crime unpunished is crime rewarded. The 1986 Immigration Reform and Control Act (IRCA) offered what was supposed to be a limited amnesty, coupled with a reinvigorated effort to enforce immigration laws. But IRCA actually created a huge influx of unassimilated migrants as newly "legalized" aliens began to import their relatives through the process of "chain immigration." At the same time, the measure's amnesty provision sent a clear signal that our government has no credible interest in enforcing our nation's immigration laws.

Thus the number of illegal aliens grew unchecked — and the 1986 IRCA amnesty eventually begat the 2004 Bush amnesty. And even as they girded up to deal with the consequences of the latest "amnesty rush," Border Patrol agents were ordered not to discuss developments that would reflect negatively on the Bush plan. A memo sent by the Customs and Border Protection headquarters in Washington ordered agents: "Do not speculate about the program. Do not provide statistics on apprehension spikes or past amnesty data."[7]

With apologies to Tennyson, these agents were told, in effect: Theirs was not to question why; theirs was but to watch our nation die. Borders, after all, are indispensable to defining national identity, as are enforceable laws, a shared language, and a common public culture. The Bush amnesty was a direct assault on all of these indispensable traits of an independent nation.

Come One, Come All

Perhaps the most remarkable thing about the Bush amnesty plan was the president's insistence that it wasn't amnesty at all. "This plan is not amnesty, placing undocumented workers on the automatic path of citizenship," insisted President Bush during a press conference with Mexican President Vicente Fox. "I oppose amnesty because it encourages the violation of our laws and perpetuates illegal immigration."[8]

But the unavoidable reality of the Bush proposal is that it would reward those who broke our immigration laws: They would be allowed to jump the queue and obtain legal status ahead of millions of people who followed our laws, many of whom spend years in their quest for citizenship.

Described as a "guest-worker" plan, the Bush amnesty proposal included:

- "legal status, as temporary workers, [for] the millions of undocumented men and women now employed in the United States, and to those in foreign countries who seek to participate in the program and have been offered employment here";
- a three-year, renewable grant of legal status;
- an increase in the annual allotment of "green cards that can lead to citizenship" for illegal aliens, and an increase in the limit on legal immigration, which President Bush insisted was "too low."[9]

In announcing his proposal, President Bush was flanked by representatives of Hispanic lobbying groups, including the rad-

ical League of United Latin American Citizens. He also referred to Tony Garza, the administration's ambassador to Mexico, as "El Embajador of Mexico" — a bizarre and puzzling
way to refer to an official who supposedly represents our nation's interests abroad.

But the entire thrust of Mr. Bush's announcement was that
America has an obligation to provide economic help to foreigners — including those who violate our nation's laws. "[Im-
migration reform] must begin by confronting a basic fact of
life and economics: some of the jobs being generated in America's growing economy are jobs American citizens are not filling," he intoned. "Out of common sense and fairness, our laws
should allow workers to enter our country and fill jobs that
Americans … are not filling.… If an American employer is offering a job that American citizens are not willing to take, we
ought to welcome into our country a person who will fill that
job." The entire purpose of our immigration system, he concluded, should be to "match willing foreign workers with willing American employers, when no Americans can be found to
fill the jobs." [10]

In reality, there are few jobs that can't attract American employees — if the price (the offered wage) is suitable. Throw-
ing open the American labor market to hordes of desperate immigrants from Mexico, Central America, the Middle East, and
Asia will artificially depress wages. The result will be either a
huge influx of low-wage foreign labor, a radical decline of living standards on the part of Americans willing to work for
Third World wages — or both.

"It's all a matter of supply and demand," points out Steve
Sailer, president of the Human Biodiversity Institute. "As they
teach you during the first week of Econ 101, when the supply
of labor goes up its price [wage] goes down.… The only re-
striction the Bush people are talking about is that the job offers to foreigners must meet the minimum wage. That's $5.15
per hour, or $10,712 for a full-time worker."

Members of the opinion-molding class are largely indifferent to these realities, Sailer notes. "Massive immigration is
vastly more popular among the elites than among the public.
Lawyers, politicians, and business executives won't find their
pay driven down much by increased competition. On the other hand, if I was, say, a carpenter, I'd be horrified by what the
President of the United States is planning to do to me and my
family. What's the global average wage made by carpenters?
I'd be surprised if it were more than 33 percent of the average
American carpenter's wage, and I wouldn't be shocked if it
were only 10 percent as much." [11]

Thus in addition to legalizing a huge pool of illegal immigrants and setting the stage for another round of "chain immigration," the Bush amnesty proposal would amount to a global job fair, with the American labor market thrown open to low-
wage workers from every nation.

With high-tech and manufacturing jobs fleeing the U.S.A.,
and millions of low-skilled workers flooding in, what will
America look like a decade from now?

Homeland Insecurity

Sailer described the Bush amnesty plan as "a globalist libertarian's fantasy. It's essentially identical to the *Wall Street Journal* editorial page's long campaign for a constitutional amend-
ment reading 'There shall be open borders.'"

Curiously, however, the Bush administration, and the globalist elites it serves, are concerned about preserving some national borders. Just not our own.

Two years after the devastating 9-11 terrorist assault on our
nation, our nation's borders remained terrifyingly insecure,
and our wounded economy continued to shed manufacturing
jobs. Assessing this grim situation, the political class in Washington focused intently on the task of rebuilding critically
wounded economic infrastructure and enhancing border security … *in Iraq*.

As annual budget deficits sagged to unprecedented depths, the Bush administration requested an emergency appropriation of $87 billion to fund the occupation and reconstruction of its war-ravaged Mesopotamian colony. $20 billion of that amount was earmarked to address "critical needs for security and infrastructure" in Iraq, such as the nation's electrical, water, sewage, and telecommunication systems, as well as housing, roads, and bridges. Hundreds of millions of dollars were to be spent on "private sector business initiatives and jobs training programs."[12]

Why American taxpayers, drowning in debt, ravaged by inflation, and anxious over their own employment prospects, should pay to train Iraqi workers, the Bush administration didn't deign to explain.

More than two million dollars was requested by Iraq's colonial administration "to fund public safety including police [and] border enforcement."[13] The Iraqi Provisional Authority pleaded for $150 million to train new Iraqi border control and customs officials, as well as to refurbish scores of border outposts.

"Without this investment," insisted the authority's request, "the nation will continue to be at tremendous risk of penetration by members of terrorist cells and other subversive organizations; smuggling will continue to bleed the revenues necessary for the Iraqi economy to stand on its own and Iraq will not be able to control its borders."[14]

In keeping with its globalist perspective, the *Wall Street Journal* — one of the key tone-setting organs of the "conservative" media — editorially endorsed the Bush administration's skewed priorities. Applauding the amnesty proposal, the *Journal* denounced the "nativist Right" for calling for drastic measures, including, if necessary, the deployment of our military to guard the southern border — "as if an already stretched Army doesn't have enough missions. Somehow draining the terror swamp in the Middle East seems a lot more vital to U.S.

security than stopping busboys from crossing the Rio Grande." [15]

Even assuming that occupying Iraq was somehow helping to drain the Middle East "terror swamp," it's difficult for rational people to see why protecting Iraq's borders is more critical to our national security than protecting our own.

One beneficiary of the 1986 IRCA amnesty was terrorist "sleeper" agent Mahmoud Abouhalima, the ringleader of the 1993 World Trade Center bombing. Co-conspirator Mohammed Salameh also applied for amnesty but was turned down — yet, perhaps in part because of the bureaucratic burden created by the amnesty, he was still able to remain in the country for seven years.

In anticipation of its amnesty plan, the Bush administration pressured financial institutions and municipal governments to accept Mexico's *matricula consular* cards as legitimate identification, despite the fact that they are issued to Mexican immigrants irrespective of their legal status. [16]

Just weeks before President Bush announced his amnesty plan, Imelda Ortiz Abdala, a former Mexican consul in Lebanon, was arrested and charged with running an immigrant-smuggling ring into the U.S. Between 1998 and 2001, Ortiz — aided by Mexican citizen Salim Boughader, a native of Lebanon — smuggled numerous individuals into the U.S., including at least one identified as a "Muslim extremist."

Ortiz's role in this scheme, allegedly, was to provide fraudulent Mexican passports (at up to $4,500 a copy) to Boughader's clients. Between 1999 and his arrest in November 2002, Boughader reportedly smuggled about 300 illegal immigrants from Lebanon into the U.S. Convicted of human trafficking last March, Boughader was released and deported to Mexico after serving 10 months. Arrested again in Mexico, Boughader now faces up to 30 years in prison on organized crime-related charges. [17]

Ironically, Boughader served time in a U.S. prison — and

faces a lengthy prison term in Mexico — for committing exactly the offenses that would be legalized by the Bush amnesty plan. And the illegal immigrant ring he created with the help of a Mexican diplomat offered a telling illustration of the potentially deadly consequences of undermining our borders.

Why Borders Matter

Even if our nation didn't face a grave threat from foreign terrorism, controlling immigration would be vital to the preservation of our free institutions.

In his report on immigration to the First Congress, James Madison urged that America "welcome every person of good fame [who] really means to incorporate himself into our society, but repel all who will not be a real addition to the wealth and strength of the United States." To reasonable people, Madison was only stating the obvious: America's immigration policies should serve the interests of our nation while preserving its prosperity, independence, free institutions, and distinctive civic culture.

Given that our nation's political system, economy, and cultural institutions are outgrowths of Anglo-European traditions, it's not surprising that for roughly the first 200 years of our national existence American immigration policies traditionally favored English-speaking immigrants from Europe who could adapt themselves to our institutions.

Ironic as it may seem to those of the statist persuasion, the absence of a welfare "safety net" was another source of social cohesion during the "great wave" of immigration that occurred between 1890 and 1920. Immigration researcher Peter Brimelow estimates, "At the turn of the century, 40 percent of all immigrants went home, basically because they failed in the work force." Millions of others, often with the help of extended families, religious institutions, and fraternal organizations, found a secure foothold in our nation. They learned our common language, adopted our public culture, and succeeded in

America's economy. Many of them, particularly those who had fled poverty, oppression, and persecution, went on to become exceptionally idealistic citizens.[18]

This isn't to say, however, that the absence of a welfare state allowed the luxury of open borders. The immigration acts of 1921 and 1924, passed largely in reaction to the social pressures accompanying the "great wave," were sought to preserve a stable status quo by imposing a national origins quota system. The McCarran-Walter Act of 1952 retained the basic structure of the 1924 measure, enhanced with provisions intended to deny admission to known subversives.[19]

The Immigration Reform Act (IRA) of 1965 completely inverted our nation's border policies by assuming that they should serve the interests of the world, rather than of our nation. Senator Robert F. Kennedy (D-N.Y.) put this proposition quite plainly during debate over the measure, insisting that "the relevant community is not merely the nation, but all men of goodwill."[20]

IRA was deliberately designed to increase immigration from non-Western nations; this was accomplished by abolishing the national origins quota system. Although the formal immigration quota was raised only slightly, the measure allowed for theoretically unlimited "non-quota" immigration for refugees, asylum seekers, and relatives of naturalized citizens for purposes of "family reunification" (by a process known as "chain immigration").

For IRA's critics, the measure's consequences — a flood tide of unassimilable immigrants and resulting social turmoil — were entirely predictable. Senator Edward Kennedy (D-Mass.), who served as Senate floor manager for the Senate version of IRA, tried to defuse those objections by offering soothing assurances of what the bill supposedly would not do:

> First, our cities will not be flooded with a million immigrants annually. Under the proposed bill, the present

Joining the "race to the bottom": Foreclosure notices paper the wall of a county courthouse in North Carolina, illustrating NAFTA's economic and social cost. The trade pact has practically destroyed North Carolina's textile industry, leaving many unemployed workers with mortgages they can't pay.

Greengrocer Steven Thoburn was prosecuted for violating European Union standards. His crime? He sold bananas by the pound instead of the EU-prescribed metric system.

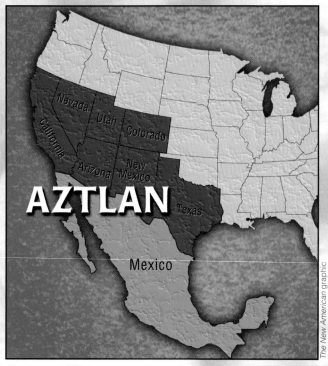

The New American graphic

Chicano militants — many of them underwritten by Establishment tax-exempt foundations, such as Ford — have demanded that the territory of "Aztlan" be returned to Mexico. The name "Aztlan" refers to the mythical homeland of the Aztec Indian. The militants seek to reverse the provisions of the 1848 Treaty of Hidalgo, which ended the Mexican War.

The official FTAA website (http://www.alca-ftaa.org/busfac/clist_e.asp) features links to all 34 of the proposed FTAA member states. Left to right, top to bottom:

Antigua and Barbuda; Argentina; Bahamas; Barbados; Belize; Bolivia; Brazil; Canada; Chile; Colombia; Costa Rica; Dominica; Dominican Republic; Ecuador; El Salvador; Grenada; Guatemala; Guyana; Haiti; Honduras; Jamaica; Mexico; Nicaragua; Panama; Paraguay; Peru; St. Kitts and Nevis; St. Lucia; St. Vincent and the Grenadines; Suriname; Trinidad and Tobago; United States; Uruguay; Venezuela.

The "Immigrant Freedom Ride" of Fall 2003 included thousands of illegal aliens marching with Communist Party agitators and labor union radicals. The demonstrators descended on the town of Doraville, Georgia, where they helped apply "pressure from below" in support of the Bush administration's proposed amnesty program for illegal aliens.

United States of MexiDa? Or CanaCo? The webpage of NAFTA's Secretariat features a composite flag combining Old Glory with Mexican and Canadian flags.

In a "Special "Davos Edition" for December 2001–February 2002, *Newsweek* international edition Managing Editor Michael Hirsh penned an article titled "The Death of a Founding Myth." In it, Hirsh wrote:

"[T]he internationalists [have] always [been] hard at work in quiet places making plans for a more perfect global community. In the end the internationalists have always dominated national policy. Even so, they haven't bragged about their globe-building for fear of reawakening the other half of the American psyche, our berserker nativism. And so they have always done it in the most out-of-the-way places and with little ado."

ISSUES 2002 TERRORISM

Farewell to isolation: The terrorist attacks permanently altered America's self-identity. We must now embrace the global community we ourselves built. BY MICHAEL HIRSH

THE DEATH OF A FOUNDING MYTH

European Union Expansion

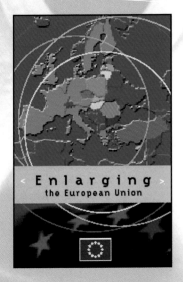

The newest EU nations (2004) appear in blue (above) and applicant states in lavender. According to "Enlarging the European Union," (left):

"The European Union is currently engaged in its most ambitious enlargement ever. The aim is to reunite the European continent and thus to consolidate peace, democracy and welfare."

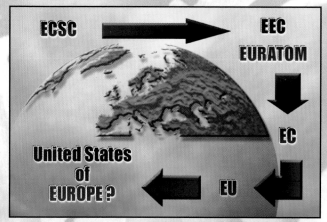

Starting with the European Coal and Steel Community in 1951, Europeans have been sold a series of so-called trade pacts which have eroded national borders. Europe has a single currency, a European Parliament, and is negotiating a European constitution.

Virtually all regional trade blocs are designed to fit into the overall structure of the United Nations. Jean Monnet, the French socialist economist and architect of the European Community, planned economic union as a stepping-stone to political union.

JBS national "STOP the FTAA" campaign makes an emphatic point. NAFTA has already had a major negative impact on the U.S. economy; FTAA will compound the problem — and threaten our very existence as a sovereign nation.

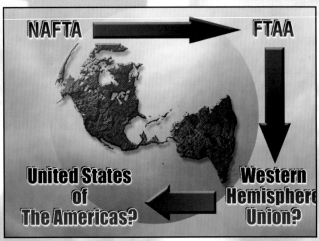

Globalist planners have designed a natural progression: from NAFTA, to the FTAA, to a Western Hemisphere without borders. A similar merger of nations is already well on its way in Europe.

level of immigration remains substantially the same....
Secondly, the ethnic mix of this country will not be up-
set.... Contrary to the charges in some quarters, [IRA]
will not inundate America with immigrants from any one
country or area, or the most populated and economically deprived nations of Africa and Asia.... In the final
analysis, the ethnic pattern of immigration under the proposed measure is not expected to change as sharply as
the critics seem to think.[21]

Not surprisingly, Peter Brimelow observes, "Every one of
Senator Kennedy's assurances has proven false. Immigration
levels did surge upward. They are now [during the mid-1990s]
running at around a million a year, not counting illegals. Immigrants do come predominantly from one area — some 85
percent of the 16.7 million legal immigrants arriving in the
United States between 1968 and 1993 came from the Third
World: 47 percent from Latin America and the Caribbean; 34
percent from Asia.... Also, immigrants did come disproportionately from one country — 20 percent from Mexico."[22] In
addition to the millions of illegal aliens who flood our shores
annually, America takes in more legal immigrants than *the rest
of the industrial world combined.*

Counter-Assimilation
It is conceivable that American society could handle even an
influx of this magnitude, if it weren't for the counter-assimilationist roles played by the welfare state and the huge racial en-
titlements industry. Liberal commentator Michael Lind, who
does not reject the welfare/affirmative action state in principle,
points out: "As a proportion of the U.S. population, the groups
eligible for racial preference benefits are rapidly growing,
thanks to mass immigration from Latin America and Asia."

While earlier European immigrants were under the necessity of assimilating quickly, Lind observes that "today's His-

panic and Asian immigrants are tempted by a variety of rewards for retaining their distinctive racial identities, even their
different languages":

> The moment a Mexican or Chinese immigrant becomes
> a naturalized citizen of the United States, he can quali-
> fy for special consideration in admission to colleges and
> universities, at the expense of better-qualified white
> Americans; expect and receive special treatment in em-
> ployment; apply for minority business subsidies denied
> to his neighbors; and even demand to have congressional
> district lines redrawn to maximize the likelihood of
> electing someone of his race or ethnic group....[23]

Building constituencies of dependents is a major industry
for any welfare state, particularly if the dependents in question are effectively confined to a cultural and linguistic ghetto. Yes, most immigrants — including those who come here
illegally — are inclined to work. Many of them, particularly
those from Mexico, work very hard.[24] But where earlier generations of immigrants had to provide for themselves — thereby learning to adapt to our country and society — the present
welfare system creates perverse incentives for separatism, at
considerable expense to the taxpayer.

In a 1993 study, economist Donald Huddle of Rice University documented that "immigrants cost the American taxpayer more than $42.5 billion in 1992 alone" for services such
as subsidized education, Medicaid, health and welfare services, bilingual education, and other benefits. The cost of welfare
subsidies to immigrants between 1993 and 2002, Huddle estimated, would average "$67 billion per year in 1992 dollars,
a net total of $668.5 billion after taxes over the decade."[25]

"Mexifornia"

California absorbs roughly 40 percent of America's immigrants — a fact that contributed significantly to the state's insolvency and recent gubernatorial recall. Although California's immigrants come from Europe, Asia, the former Soviet Union, the Caribbean, and various Latin American nations, simple geography dictates that the largest percentage — especially those who come illegally — arrive from Mexico.

"Most arrivals are given work by grateful employers," notes Victor Davis Hanson, a professor of classics and farmer who lives in northern California. "Although illegal aliens are eager to get a fighting chance to succeed in America, many are not prepped for, nor immersed into, the cutthroat competitive culture they help to mobilize. Instead, in recent years they and their offspring have ended up in ethnic enclaves of the mind and barrios of the flesh. In these locations they often soon become dependent on subsidies — and too many of their children will join an underclass to be led by ethnic shepherds who often do more harm than good...."[26]

Counter-assimilationist pressures abound in California. Many of Hanson's most outstanding students are Americans of Mexican ancestry. Fluent in English and appreciative of our nation's free institutions, those students eagerly learn of our culture's heritage and literature — only to find themselves ostracized by many of their peers for displaying inadequate devotion to *La Raza* ("the race"). Hanson records that his "Mexican-American students, even those of nearly 100 percent Indian heritage, face hostility from their own ethnic communities when they assimilate, speak perfect English, and prefer Latin and Greek literature to Chicano studies...."[27]

This embittered, militant separatism has been carefully cultivated by the state's political and economic establishment. "The Mexican-American caucus in the legislature demands that state universities, by fiat, graduate Hispanics at rates commensurate with the surrounding community's racial makeup," notes Hanson. "Right and Left, working in an uneasy partnership that trumps traditional political affinities, lobby for open borders to allow millions to come north. The *Wall Street Journal* and Chicano studies departments often agree on open borders.... The two parties, for reasons of money and power, ignore the social chaos brought by millions of illegal aliens: capitalists count on profits from plentiful, cheap workers, while activists expect these laborers to become liberal voters." [28]

Although this growing pool of "cheap labor" might seem attractive, it actually incurs substantial costs: As of 2003, the average California household was required to pay $1,200 a year to make up the difference between the cost of welfare payments to immigrants and the amount they pay in taxes. "Wages to illegals are often paid in cash, which is a bargain for everyone involved," notes Hanson. "For instance, at $10 an hour without state, federal and payroll taxes deducted, the worker really earns the equivalent of a gross $13 an hour or more, while the employer saves over 30 percent in payroll contributions and expensive paperwork. Meanwhile, however, such cash payments force other Americans and legal immigrants to pay steeper taxes in part to cover those who pay none. So the farmer cheering over access to solid, dependable, cheap labor is now learning that he pays more than he thinks for illegal aliens in the form of rising taxes as well as a fraying social fabric." [29]

Not only are law-abiding Californians forced to subsidize law-breakers, they are also touched up to create a multi-generational indigent class. At age 50, notes Brimelow, "the illegal worker is physically worn out and unemployable. His American-born children are alienated high-school dropouts. More illegals arrive to do the work that [American citizens] 'won't do.' The cycle of privatized profits and socialized costs begins anew." [30]

"My once sleepy hometown of Selma, California, in the center of the San Joaquin Valley, is ... in the middle of all this," comments Hanson:

On our streets I have no idea whether the mostly young

male illegal aliens I meet are economic refugees or fugitives from crime in Mexico, perhaps serious felons — and no one else does either, because there is no legal record of their existence, and what documents they and our local authorities possess are almost always fraudulent, forged to mask the conditions of their arrival.... Selma is now somewhere between 60 and 90 percent Hispanic.... At the gas station a mile away from our farm, I rarely hear English spoken. Almost every car of immigrants that pulls in displays a Mexican flag decal somewhere."[31]

La Reconquista

California, warns Hanson, is a harbinger of radical changes being engineered in our nation's culture and political system as we are overrun by "the most uneducated and destitute of the entire North American subcontinent," a process that conjures "a looming nightmare of unassimilated Third-Worldism."[32]

Mexico is ruled by a deeply entrenched oligarchy that — as former Mexican Foreign Minister Jorge Castaneda admits — uses emigration to the United States as a social "safety valve."[33] While Mexico eagerly exports its surplus poverty northward, it ferociously guards its southern border.

In 2001, the Mexican government conducted an ambitious program called "Plan Sur," intended to seal off Mexico's 600-mile frontier with Guatemala and Belize, as well as the Isthmus of Tehuantepec. In 2000 and 2001, Mexico deported more than a quarter-million illegal immigrants from Central and South America. According to Felipe de Jesus Preciado, head of the Mexican migration service, "the flow of Central American migrants north is a national security problem for Mexico. It wouldn't be such a big problem if they were getting through to the U.S., but they get stuck and hang around in the frontier cities making trouble, sleeping in the streets with no money."[34]

From the Mexican regime's perspective, the United States

has a duty not only to absorb whatever portion of the Mexican population it chooses to send our way, but also to relieve Mexico's own problem with illegal immigration by keeping the borders open to Central American immigrants as well.

While President George W. Bush pointedly referred to Mexico as "our good friend," the Mexican government could be considered a potentially dangerous adversary. Communist China is more powerful, North Korea is better-armed, and "post-Soviet" Russia remains deeply involved in fomenting subversion and terrorism world-wide. But apart from Mexico, no other foreign power is actively carrying out a plan to occupy and "re-conquer" U.S. territory. Mexico's government actually claims to represent not only its expatriate nationals within our borders — whether here legally or illegally — but also *Americans of Mexican ancestry who were born here and have never set foot in Mexico.* And the Mexican ruling elite exploits every opportunity to cultivate public hostility toward the United States.

"Mexican newspaper readers and television viewers are regaled constantly with descriptions of the ill-treatment of Mexicans in the United States," observes Alan Wall, an American citizen who works as a teacher in Mexico. "America's attempts to control its own borders are presented as 'racist,' 'xenophobic,' and 'anti-Mexican.' The United States is blamed for deaths of illegal aliens who die crossing the border in the desert, and Mexican politicians have called the border a 'slaughterhouse' and a 'modern Nazi zone.' "[35]

"In Mexico, all political parties support increased Mexican emigration to the United States, amnesty [for illegal aliens], and government benefits for Mexicans in the United States," Wall continues. "In fact, very few influential Mexicans publicly acknowledge the right of the U.S. to control her own borders. Mexican illegal aliens 'are not criminals,' 'they only do the work the gringos won't do,' and 'they are obliged to cross the border' — these are common slogans used to justify illegal emigration."[36]

Many prominent Mexicans openly speak of *La Reconquista* — "re-conquest" — of the southwestern United States, portions of which were (for a short time) Mexican territories during the early 19th century.

In an article published more than two decades ago in *Excelsior*, the Mexican analogue to the *New York Times*, columnist Carlos Loret de Mola described the outpouring of Mexican immigrants into the United States as "The Great Invasion":

> A peaceful mass of people … carries out slowly and patiently an unstoppable invasion, the most important in human history. You cannot give me a similar example of such a large migratory wave by an ant-like multitude, stubborn, unarmed, and carried on in the face of the most powerful and best-armed nation on earth.... [Neither] barbed-wire fences, nor aggressive border guards, nor campaigns, nor laws, nor police raids against the undocumented, have stopped this movement of the masses that is unprecedented in any part of the world.[37]

According to Loret, the migrant invasion "seems to be slowly returning [the southwestern United States] to the jurisdiction of Mexico without the firing of a single shot, nor requiring the least diplomatic action, by means of a steady, spontaneous, and uninterrupted occupation."

The notion that those U.S. territories are "returning to the jurisdiction of Mexico" is an allusion to the concept that California, Arizona, New Mexico, Colorado, and Texas, the states created in the territory obtained from Mexico through the Treaty of Guadalupe Hidalgo in 1848, compose "Aztlan," the mythical homeland of the Aztec Indian.

For decades, Chicano militants — many of them underwritten by Establishment tax-exempt foundations, such as Ford — have demanded that the territory of "Aztlan" be taken back from the United States. Among the most radical of these groups are the campus-based *Movimiento Estudiantil de Chicanos de Aztlan* (MEChA), the Mexican-American Legal Defense and Education Fund (MALDEF), the National Council of La Raza, and the League of United Latin American Citizens (LULAC).[38]

These groups are all tightly linked with the Mexican government as well.[39] During a June 2001 address to the annual convention of LULAC, Jorge Castaneda praised the group for its efforts to lobby Washington on behalf of the Mexican government, and (according to an account in the Mexican press) "urged LULAC convention-goers to lobby U.S. legislators to push for immigration accords."[40]

Under President Vicente Fox, the Mexican government created a cabinet-level office called the National Council for Mexicans Abroad. Headed by an official who has dual citizenship in the U.S. and Mexico, the council's purpose, according to Fox, was to act as a liaison between the Mexican President and the "23 million Mexicans in the U.S." That number includes American citizens of Mexican ancestry.[41]

Mexico uses its 48 consulates on U.S. soil to meddle in our domestic politics and mobilize Mexican-Americans on behalf of a foreign government. In 1994, Mexico's consulate in Los Angeles helped organize resistance to Proposition 187, a ballot measure seeking to deny non-emergency welfare benefits to illegal aliens. In Houston, the Mexican consul — along with officials from the U.S. Department of Labor, the Equal Employment Opportunity Commission, and the radical group MALDEF — participated in a consortium to educate and advise immigrants who consider themselves victims of discrimination in matters of immigration, employment, or wages. Teodoro Maus, Mexican consul-general in Atlanta, publicly opposed designation of English as Georgia's official language. He also led campaigns to reprimand local political leaders and even radio talk-show hosts whose comments were deemed "anti-Mexican."[42]

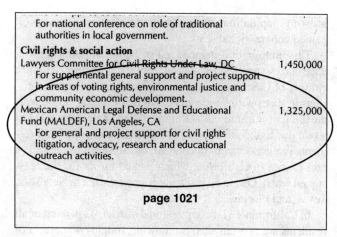

For national conference on role of traditional
authorities in local government.

Civil rights & social action

Lawyers Committee for Civil Rights Under Law, DC   1,450,000
  For supplemental general support and project support
  in areas of voting rights, environmental justice and
  community economic development.

Mexican American Legal Defense and Educational   1,325,000
Fund (MALDEF), Los Angeles, CA
  For general and project support for civil rights
  litigation, advocacy, research and educational
  outreach activities.

page 1021

The Foundation 1000 1999/2000 directory shows a typical Ford Foundation grant of $1,325,000 to MALDEF — a radical group promoting "Aztlan."

Electing a New People

Although the impact of unchecked immigration from Mexico is felt primarily in the southwestern U.S., it has had an unmistakable — and largely ignored — impact on our nation's political landscape. Illegal immigration has distorted the electoral map by re-distributing seats in the House of Representatives.

Apportionment of congressional seats is based on census figures, which include (sometimes through the use of dubious "statistical sampling" methods) illegal immigrants. The results from the 2000 census caused Indiana, Michigan, and Mississippi to lose a congressional seat; Montana, which has long had a single seat, failed to acquire a second one, as had been expected; Oklahoma, Pennsylvania, Wisconsin, Kentucky, and Utah also had one fewer congressional seat than they would have were it not for the presence of "non-citizens." California, New York, Florida, and Texas — each of which has a large and growing population of unassimilated alien migrants — all gained congressional seats.[43]

This immigration-induced redistribution of political influence "takes away representation from states composed almost entirely of U.S. citizens and results in the creation of new districts in states with large numbers of non-citizens," comments the Center for Immigration Reform. "In the nine states that lost a seat due to the presence of non-citizens, only one in 50 residents is a non-citizen. In contrast, one in seven residents is a non-citizen in California, which picked up six [of the reassigned seats]. One in 10 residents is a non-citizen in New York, Texas, and Florida...."[44]

In California's 31st congressional district, 43 percent of all residents are non-citizens. Nationwide, roughly 40 percent of all Hispanics are non-citizens. As commentator John J. Miller observes, packing them into congressional districts threatens to re-create the notorious "rotten boroughs" of 18th century England, in which only a handful of people were eligible to vote. "Non-citizen apportionment has delivered something very much like this to our own shores, though we might call them 'rotten barrios,' " states Miller.[45]

Thanks in some measure to the influence of "rotten barrios," the electoral landscape for presidential politics will be altered, since votes in the Electoral College are based on the size of congressional delegations. During the run-up to the 1996 presidential elections, the Clinton administration took a more direct approach to altering the landscape by hurriedly naturalizing more than one million immigrants in politically critical states.

Through the "Citizenship USA" program, administered by Vice President Al Gore, hundreds of thousands of applicants for naturalization were rushed through the naturalization process "in disregard of normal procedures and legal standards, such as criminal background checks," recalls former Congressman Bob Barr. This "allowed a flood of immigrants

to gain citizenship without meeting the standard INS procedures." Nearly 180,000 immigrants, including an estimated
11,000 with prior felony arrests, were made citizens without
undergoing required FBI background checks. An INS depor-
tation officer who had left the Citizenship USA program in
disgust complained to the *Chicago Tribune*: "They are not
stopping people the way we used to. The big initiative is to get
all these people eligible to vote and registered. It's just a rush
for numbers."[46]

This cynical effort to undermine our national identity in
search of political advantage brings to mind Berthold Brecht's
sarcastic reaction to East Germany's 1953 crackdown on labor unrest: "If the government doesn't like the people, why
doesn't it dissolve them and elect a new people?" Obviously,
the immediate political beneficiaries of unchecked immigration are the architects and custodians of the welfare state. But
it shouldn't be thought that liberal Democrats are alone in their
enthusiasm for open borders.

Merging with Mexico

"Whatever else George W. Bush does, or doesn't do," commented *Newsweek* political analyst Howard Fineman in late
2001, "he has earned a place in history as the first American
president to place Hispanic voters at the center of politics, and
the first to view the land between Canada and Guatemala as
one. It makes sense, if you think about it: Texas, long ago and
far away, was part of Mexico. Now a Texan is trying to re-
assemble the Old Country, and then some."[47]

Fineman's history is rather faulty. Texas was "part of Mexico" in the same sense that the Thirteen American Colonies
were "part" of England. Like the American Colonists, the
"Texicans" fought a war of independence that grew out of an
effort to vindicate their constitutional rights (in their case,
rights promised under Mexico's 1824 constitution). Texas was-
n't part of the "Old Country" when it was admitted to the

Union, but rather an independent republic. But Fineman was absolutely right in saying that the policy promoted by the Bush administration was to amalgamate the entire hemisphere.

During the August 2001 state visit of Vicente Fox to the United States, President Bush convened a meeting of the U.S.-Mexico Binational Commission, a cabinet-level body in which officials from both national governments develop joint policies on such issues as immigration, counter-narcotics efforts, trade, energy, and foreign policy.[48] In 1993, under the NAFTA framework, the U.S. and Mexico established the Border Environment Cooperation Commission and the North American Development Bank (NADBank).

Although the NADBank was originally designed to finance environmental initiatives at the border, the Fox administration demanded to use the bank to subsidize projects "in non-environmental sectors and in a wider geographic zone," to use the delicate language of a White House press release. In an interview published in the September 4, 2001 *Washington Post,* Fox claimed that using the NADBank to subsidize economic development in Mexico is justified by the "broad spirit of cooperation, as well as justice and equity." This is to say that Mexico sees NADBank as a U.S. taxpayer-subsidized piñata.

But this isn't all. During Fox's visit the *Atlanta Journal-Constitution* noted that Fox "envisions a North American economic alliance that will make the border between the United States and Mexico as unrestricted as the one between Tennessee and Georgia."[49] Of course, Tennessee and Georgia are not separate, independent countries, but states in the same constitutional union. This implies that the United States and Mexico, as well as Canada, would cede their sovereignty to a new, supra-national political union — a prospect warmly endorsed by the *Journal-Constitution.*

"The ultimate goal of any White House policy ought to be a North American economic and political alliance similar in scope and ambition to the European Union," opined a *Jour-*

nal-Constitution house editorial for September 7th. "Unlike the varied landscapes and cultures of European Union members, the United States, Canada and Mexico already share a great deal in common, and language is not as great a barrier. President Bush, for example, is quite comfortable with the blended Mexican-Anglo culture forged in the border states of Texas, California and Arizona."[50]

"Fundamentally, economic integration with Mexico is inevitable," insists Jagdish Sheth of Emory University. Speaking of U.S.-Mexico convergence, Georgia State University economist David Sjoquist declares: "Our choice is to fight it and lose, or embrace it and come out better for it."[51]

Essentially, this is the "argument from inevitability," a tactic preferred by rapists seeking to minimize their victims' resistance: "It's going to happen anyway, so you might as well hold still and enjoy it." President Bush preferred to dress up that argument with a layer of humanitarian gloss: "There are people in Mexico who've got children, who worry about where they're going to get their next meal from," asserted the president. "And they're going to come to the United States.... That's a simple fact. And we've got to respect that...."[52]

But as noted above, the hardship of ordinary Mexicans is largely the result of that nation's embedded criminal ruling elite, which uses emigration to the U.S. as a means of forestalling desperately needed reforms. That elite has been supported for decades by U.S. foreign policy and foreign aid. If the intent is to make life better for Mexico's long-suffering people, turning the U.S. into a combination public works project/welfare hostel for Mexicans won't work. It will, however, succeed in "harmonizing" America down to Mexico's economic level.

During their 2001 summit, presidents Bush and Fox laid the groundwork for the so-called "Partnership for Prosperity" (PfP) — an initiative designed to use American tax dollars to build Mexico's manufacturing sector. Like most international socialist undertakings of this sort, the PfP was formally inaugurated at a UN global conference — specifically, the March 2002 UN foreign aid conference in Monterrey, Mexico. According to the U.S. State Department, PfP's action plan calls for U.S. assistance in Mexico to boost investment in housing and commercial infrastructure to boost Mexican productivity.

A key outgrowth of the PfP was a bilateral agreement signed in June of 2002 to permit the Overseas Private Investment Corporation (OPIC) "to offer all its programs and services in Mexico...." OPIC was established by Congress to help U.S. companies invest overseas by granting direct loans or loan guarantees for investments and extending insurance to cover the risks of investment. CEO Peter S. Watson boasted that the bilateral agreement with Mexico "will help to further unleash the entrepreneurial capacity of Mexican businesses by mobilizing U.S. capital, and consequently bring important developmental benefits to the Mexican people.... [It] will also allow OPIC to work freely along with its sister agencies, the US Trade and Development Agency and the Export Import Bank of the US, in providing investment support in Mexico...."[53]

In brief, OPIC and its sister agencies are using taxpayer money, and the full faith and credit of the U.S. government, to promote the relocation of manufacturing jobs from the U.S. to Mexico — even as Washington keeps both our borders and the welfare spigots open to invaders from the south.

"The Whole Enchilada, or Nothing"
Within the framework for the PfP, presidents Bush and Fox pledged that they would "strive to consolidate a North American economic community whose benefits reach the lesser-developed areas of the region and extend to the most vulnerable social groups in our countries."[54]

Within a few months of that declaration, the Mexican government had composed a five-point program to hasten "consolidation" with the U.S.:

- Legalization of "undocumented" workers (that is, illegal aliens from Mexico);
- An expanded permanent visas program;
- An enhanced guest-worker visas program;
- Border control cooperation;
- Economic development in immigrant-sending regions of Mexico.

This list of demands, according to Mexican foreign minister Jorge Castaneda, was essentially non-negotiable: He insisted that the U.S. had to accept "the whole enchilada, or nothing." [55]

The problem, of course, is that there was nothing for the U.S. on that list, apart from empty assurances of "border control cooperation" from Mexico City. In exchange for that useless promise, the U.S. was expected to grant amnesty to illegal immigrants, take on a new wave of legal resident aliens, and lavish economic aid on Mexico.

Incredible as it may seem, the Bush administration was on board. Through the PfP, taxpayers in our country were being shaken down to underwrite economic development south of the border. Amnesty for illegal aliens was all but a done deal.

Then came 9/11. For more than a year after Black Tuesday, the amnesty proposal rested on the proverbial back burner. But in July 2003, three Republican members of Arizona's congressional delegation — Senator John McCain, and Congressmen Jim Kolbe and Jeff Flake — took up the proposal anew by introducing "guest-worker" bills intended to legalize illegal immigrants currently employed in the U.S. The envisioned guest-worker program would essentially allow the entire illegal alien population in this country to apply for permanent legal residency (provided that the applicant had an employer or family sponsor). There would also be no limit to the number of "guest workers" admitted annually.

In short, the measure was designed to reward those who violated our nation's immigration laws, while effectively de-

molishing any remaining limit on legal immigration. President
Bush, head of an administration so concerned about the security of Iraq's borders, reportedly told Senator McCain and
Reps. Kolbe and Flake that he was "enthusiastic" about the
guest worker program, and that enactment of the program
would be a "high priority."[56]

To complement the amnesty proposal "from above," the
radical left organized a nationwide protest intended to demonstrate pressure "from below." Dubbed the "Immigrant Workers Freedom Ride," the Fall 2003 campaign was "reminiscent
of the civil rights struggles of the 1960s," claimed the *Atlanta
Journal-Constitution*. The protest attracted busloads of "rid-
ers" — most of them from Mexico, Central America, and
Colombia — who converged on Washington, D.C., before
heading to a final rally in New York City. A delegation from
the event paid a visit to Atlanta to lay a wreath at the grave of
Martin Luther King Jr., thereby symbolically claiming the slain
activist's mantle.

"The campaign is calling for immigration reform that will
open a path for legalization for immigrants already here, permit their families in foreign countries to join them, and protect the rights of workers, regardless of their legal status," reported the paper. "The campaign is supported by a coalition of
labor unions, religious groups and civil rights activists."[57]

Arguably the most critical omission in the *Journal-Constitution* story had to do with the role of the Communist Party
and other subversive groups in organizing the "Immigrant
Workers Freedom Ride": The event's website conspicuously
listed the Communist Party, U.S.A. among its sponsors and
provided a link to the party's website.[58] It's impossible to believe that the paper, or any similar mainstream media organ,
would decline to mention the involvement of (for example) the
Ku Klux Klan in a similar campaign.

The advertised purpose of the "Freedom Ride" was to demand that illegal immigrants in this country receive immedi-

ate amnesty for breaking our nation's laws — and be allowed to bring in their extended families in the name of "family re-unification." This process could conceivably result in our nation being inundated by *tens of millions* of unassimilated foreigners. Indeed, this has happened before.

In 1977, then-president Jimmy Carter declared that "human rights" considerations dictated a general amnesty for foreigners illegally in the United States — a population then numbering in the millions. That radical proposal was endorsed in 1980 by a special commission on immigration headed by Theodore Hesburgh: The panel recommended a general amnesty for illegal aliens, coupled with employer sanctions and a modest increase in funding for border enforcement. Those recommendations were incorporated into the Immigration Reform and Control Act of 1986 (IRCA), which was sold to an anxious American public as a definitive "solution" to the crisis of illegal immigration. But rather than mitigating the immigration onslaught, IRCA simply abetted it by opening up the process of "chain immigration" — and sending a potent signal that our borders could be violated with impunity.

One Nation, Under NAFTA/FTAA

Shortly after the conclusion of the Fall 2003 "Freedom Ride," representatives of the radical groups sponsoring that demonstration were brought to Washington by Senator John McCain (R-Ariz.) and several of his colleagues to lobby directly for passage of the disguised amnesty measure.[59] Mexican president Vicente Fox did his part by visiting three southwestern states — Texas, Arizona, and New Mexico — to lobby state legislatures to support the amnesty drive.

"We share nation and language," Fox told the New Mexico legislature. "In addition to our geographical vicinity, we are united by inseparable bonds, history, values and interests.... We must join together.... You need Mexico and Mexicans, and we need you." Acting as the supposed leader of "Mexicans living abroad," Fox demanded that lawmakers in this country "facilitate access to health care and education services for all those who share our border.... Without this, it is impossible to think about the path to greater integration and shared prosperity."[60]

Open borders, amnesty for illegals, subsidies for Mexico's economy, exporting manufacturing capacity south of the border, expanded welfare benefits for foreigners who entered our nation illegally — these are all part of the same seamless design. As Fox himself put it, that design is the "integration" of the U.S. and Mexico into a hemisphere-wide political unit.

Foreign affairs analyst Robert D. Kaplan points out that "the tumultuous historic consolidation of Mexico and the United States" is just one facet of a process of "global political convergence" into a "kind of loose world governance...." As "these two vastly unequal societies [the United States and Mexico] integrate at breakneck speed," the immediate result will be "social upheaval on both sides of the border."[61]

"Social upheaval" is a remarkably antiseptic term to describe the loss of our national identity, the importation of criminals and welfare parasites, the depression of our labor markets and exportation of our manufacturing capacity, and the forcible "downward harmonization" of our living standard with that of Mexico. But from the perspective of the globalist elite — a view that Kaplan enthusiastically shares — this is simply the price that must be paid to bring about a unified world.

CHAPTER SIX

What Can We Do?

[E]nergetic and creative individuals in government, in- terest groups, and corporations are quietly assembling global arrangements.... For the most part, they work out- side of legislatures and parliaments and are screened from the glare of the media in order to find common in- terests, shape a consensus, and persuade those with power to change.

— Harvard Business School professor George C. Lodge[1]

[T]he internationalists [have] always [been] hard at work in quiet places making plans for a more perfect global community. In the end the internationalists have always dominated national policy. Even so, they haven't bragged about their globe-building for fear of reawak- ening the other half of the American psyche, our berserker nativism. And so they have always done it in the most out-of-the-way places and with little ado.

— *Newsweek* International Edition managing editor Michael Hirsh, "The Death of a Founding Myth"[2]

When bad men combine, the good must associate; else they will fall one by one, an unpitied sacrifice in a con- temptible struggle.

— Edmund Burke[3]

Is our nation's decline foreordained and inevitable? Must the United States of America replay the sad history of previous republics that have descended into empire, impoverishment, and ruin? Do impersonal, irresistible historical trends dictate

the eclipse of our nation — its culture, institutions, and traditions — by a new global order?

The answer to all of these questions is a resounding "no."
Even without the deliberate, covertly organized efforts of pow-
er-seeking individuals, every free society can succumb to the
corruption that is an unavoidable aspect of the fallen human
condition. And it's certainly true that many of our problems
and challenges have little if anything to do with the machinations of the shadowy collective entity referred to in these pages
as the Power Elite.

Nonetheless, as we have seen, that Elite has carefully and
deliberately undertaken to undermine the American middle
class and subvert our national independence. These developments are not a result of blind, impersonal historical forces, or
of innocent errors, honest mistakes, or lapses in judgment on
the part of our leaders. Neither is our decline largely the unfortunate outcome in a long-running *ideological* conflict between liberty and collectivism.

Simply put: Our prosperity, liberty, and national independence are being stolen from us by those who seek total power
over the entire globe.

What we confront is a deliberate plot to "harmonize" our
standard of living with that of other nations and "integrate" the
United States into a centrally directed global economy, ruled
by an entrenched and unaccountable transnational Power Elite.
As illustrated by the foregoing quotes — and the evidence provided in the previous chapters — this campaign is often
shrouded by secrecy, and always involves a deliberate effort
to deceive the public. In other words, it is, by strict and specific definition, a conspiracy.

Why Conspiracy Matters

Contemporary Americans are somewhat schizoid on the subject of conspiracy. The concept is practically ubiquitous in our
literature and entertainment. Prime-time television, for in-

stance, is awash in "police procedurals" and similar crime dramas built on conspiracy plots. The same is true of movies, novels, and other diversions. When it comes to fiction, the American public has no problem accepting the concept of conspiracy.

Public opinion surveys also suggest that most Americans perceive our government to be controlled by a Power Elite. *The State of Disunion*, a nationwide survey conducted by the Congressional Institute, found that 80 percent of those polled agreed that "our country is run by a close network of special interests, public officials, and the media," and that the government itself "is pretty much run by a few big interests looking out for themselves."[4] 64 percent consider our ruling elite as amoral, indifferent to the public's concerns, and devoted exclusively to pursuing its own interests and agenda.[5]

Yet only 24 percent — less than one-quarter — of Americans surveyed were willing to say that this powerful, corrupt, well-entrenched elite is "involved in a conspiracy." Perhaps it should be considered predictable, then, that 60 percent of the respondents concluded that "people like me don't have any say about what the government does."[6] From that fatalistic perspective, government corruption is simply an unalterable reality of life, as fixed and immutable as the laws of gravity.

There is an important and sobering lesson here: A conspiracy cannot be defeated unless it is recognized, and opposed, as such. If Americans are seriously concerned about building a better life for themselves and their children, and they understand that our own government is controlled by corrupt, conniving men determined to enrich themselves at the expense of our liberty and prosperity, then it follows that those schemers and their designs must be exposed, opposed, and defeated. And this inescapably requires identifying our enemy as a conspiracy.

Think of it this way: How many large-scale crimes are committed by lone individuals? While solitary thugs are responsible for much of the violence that plagues society, the most serious damage is perpetrated by criminal syndicates — whether they're small-scale street gangs, drug smuggling rings, or vast underground empires. All of those criminal enterprises are, by strict definition, conspiracies, and unless they are investigated and prosecuted as such, they can't be defeated.

Consider the case of *La Cosa Nostra* — the multi-generational, international criminal syndicate more commonly known as the Mafia. As late as the early to mid-1980s, some "respectable" opinion still maintained that the Mafia was a figment of paranoid imagination. "There does not exist, nor has there ever existed, an organized, secret, hierarchical criminal society called 'Mafia,'" pontificated Italian scholar Pino Arlacchi in 1983.[7] In 1985, Virgil Peterson, a presidential consultant on organized crime and former head of Chicago's Crime Commission, dismissed as a "myth" the idea that the American Cosa Nostra "is controlled by a mystical and somewhat romantic Sicilian Mafia with secret initiation rites...."[8]

As defectors from the Mafia began to come forward, they were greeted with scorn and derision — or worse — from pseudo-sophisticates in powerful academic, law enforcement, and political posts. In the early 1950s, as the Senate investigated Mafia activities, Harvard sociologist Daniel Bell dismissed the inquiry, claiming that it had been "misled by its own hearsay." Twenty years later, Mafia defector Leonardo Vitale testified against several of the conspiracy's highest leaders — only to have an Italian jury dismiss his testimony and consign him to a lunatic asylum for a decade. Shortly after Vitale was released from his unjust imprisonment, he was gunned down in the streets of Palermo.[9]

The chief obstacle to dealing with the Mafia, complained Senator Estes Kefauver, a resolute enemy of the syndicate, was that for most Americans the idea of such a vast, long-lived, international conspiracy was "so fantastic that most Americans have difficulty in believing it really exists." This public disbelief was abetted by the obstinate refusal of public officials to recognize the existence of the Mafia conspiracy, and to fight it as such. "No 'friends of the friends' in the Mafia sense could have served it so well as these upright, obstinate disbelievers," commented scholar Claire Sterling. "Their refusal to see the plain truth was worse than misleading; it effectively blocked any assault on the Mafia as *an organized criminal body* for over a century."[10]

This began to change in the 1970s and 1980s when law enforcement finally began to fight the Mafia as an identifiable conspiracy. Once the secrecy — and cultivated disbelief — that had shielded the Mafia conspiracy was dispelled, the cabal itself was decimated within two decades.

Corrupt Government as a Racket

The fate of the Mafia conspiracy has more relevance to our present circumstances than merely illustrating how "respectable" opinion can be wrong. When governments become corrupt, they take on the characteristics of criminal syndicates.

As St. Augustine observed more than a millennium and a half ago in his treatise *The City of God*: "Justice being taken away, what are kingdoms but vast robberies?" Emancipated from the rule of law, and stripped of its humanitarian pretensions, government simply becomes an engine of plunder, oppression, and — ultimately — mass murder. In brief, corrupt governments become conspiracies against the liberties, property, and even the lives, of their subjects.

The American Founders — men of learning, accomplishment, courage, and vision — understood these sobering realities. Their heroic campaign to win independence from Great Britain, and later to build a constitutional republic, began with the understanding that they were battling a determined conspiracy seeking to use government power to reduce the American colonists to slavery.

In his Pulitzer Prize-winning study of the ideological foundations of American independence, Harvard historian Bernard Bailyn noted that "the fear of a comprehensive conspiracy against liberty throughout the English-speaking world — a conspiracy believed to have been nourished in corruption, and of which, it was felt, oppression in America was only the most immediately visible part — lay at the heart of the Revolutionary movement." The leaders of the drive for independence "saw about them, with increasing clarity, not merely mistaken, or even evil, policies violating the principles upon which freedom rested, but nothing less than a deliberate assault launched surreptitiously by plotters against liberty."[11]

British philosopher John Locke was among those whose wisdom inspired our Founders. In his *Second Treatise on Government*, Locke presented a useful distinction between commonplace governmental inefficiency and corruption on the one hand, and the malevolent design of conspirators bent on destroying liberty, on the other:

> Great mistakes in the ruling part, many wrong and inconvenient laws, and all the slips of human frailty will be borne by the people without mutiny or murmur. But if a long train of abuses, prevarications, and artifices, all tending the same way, *make the design visible to the people*, and they cannot but feel what they lie under and see whither they are going, it is not to be wondered that they should then rouse themselves and endeavor to put the rule into such hands which may secure to them the ends for which government was at first erected...." (Emphasis added).[12]

As the familiar aphorism puts it: Even a dumb dog can distinguish between being stumbled over and being kicked.

One key to discerning conspiracy, according to Locke, is consistency — a series of policies and decisions that have the common tendency to enslave and impoverish a government's subjects. Those trends suggest a "design," secretly arrived at and pursued through deception — in brief, a conspiracy. The Founders, applying this wisdom to their circumstances, recognized that the enemy they confronted was a conspiracy against their liberties.

Writing on behalf of the pro-revolutionary cause in 1774, John Adams declared that "the conspiracy [against the liberties of the colonists] was first regularly formed and begun to be executed in 1763 or 4...."[13]

In an essay published that same year, Thomas Jefferson endorsed Adams' perception, and pointed out that British policies toward the colonies displayed a conspiratorial pattern. While "single acts of tyranny may be ascribed to the accidental opinion of a day," Jefferson advised, "a series of oppressions, begun at a distinguished period, and pursued unalterably through every change of ministers, too plainly prove a deliberate and systematical plan of reducing us to slavery."[14]

After initially seeking to vindicate their "ancient rights as Englishmen" as subjects of the British Crown, the Founders eventually came to realize that they could only do so as citizens of free and independent states. The *Declaration of Independence*, invoking Locke's anti-conspiratorial language, asserted that separation from Great Britain was made necessary because "a long train of abuses and usurpations, pursuing invariably the same Object, evinces a design to reduce [us] under absolute Despotism...."

America's independence was thus a triumph of the anti-conspiratorial worldview, as is our Constitution. Dr. Bailyn — a liberal academic who holds no brief for "conspiracy theorists" — was compelled by his research to conclude that "the American Constitution is the final and climactic expression of the ideology of the American Revolution" — an ideology that he described as anti-conspiratorial.[15]

America's Founders would have no difficulty recognizing that there is a conspiracy behind the unfolding campaign to eradicate the middle class and absorb our nation into a centrally ruled global regime. Yet they would not have to rely on circumstantial evidence to form such a conclusion.

Controlling the Alternatives

Just as there were key Mafia insiders who blew the whistle on that criminal syndicate, former Insiders have exposed the workings of the Power Elite. The most important of those figures is the late Georgetown University political scientist Carroll Quigley — an academic recognized as a mentor by (of all people) Bill Clinton, who used his 1992 nomination acceptance speech to laud Quigley before a world audience.

In his monumental study *Tragedy and Hope*, Quigley offers a relatively brief but priceless examination of the role in modern history played by the Power Elite — a self-perpetuating international clique bent on dominating the world. Having examined that cabal's intimate documents, Quigley approved of its objectives, taking issue only with its determination to avoid publicizing its stealthy pursuit of global hegemony:

> I know of the operations of this network because I have studied it for twenty years and was permitted for two years, in the early 1960's, to examine its papers and secret records. I have no aversion to it or to most of its aims and have, for much of my life, been close to it and to many of its instruments.... In general, my chief difference of opinion is that it wishes to remain unknown.... [The network's objective is] nothing less than to create a world system of financial control in private hands able to dominate the political system of each country and the economy of the world as a whole. This system was to be controlled in a feudalist fashion by the central banks of the world acting in concert by secret meetings and conferences. The apex of the system was to be ... a private bank owned and controlled by the world's central banks

which were themselves private corporations. Each central bank ... sought to dominate its government by its ability to control treasury loans, to manipulate foreign exchanges, to influence the level of economic activity in the country, and to influence cooperative politicians by subsequent economic rewards in the business world.[16]

According to Thomas Jefferson's indictment, the conspiracy against the colonies made itself known through "a series of oppressions, begun at a distinguished period, and pursued unalterably through every change of ministers...." The effort to create the centrally controlled economy described by Quigley has displayed similar consistency. That program — which would require reversing our national independence, and reducing our middle class to peonage — has continued unchecked for at least a century, and has been pursued through every change of administration, whether Republican or Democrat.

This isn't a case of globalist, big government Democrats versus conservative, nationalist Republicans. Rather, it's the operation of a powerful, entrenched elite that effectively controls the leadership of both major parties.

Toward the end of his voluminous study, Professor Quigley — who, remember, shared the Power Elite's objectives — offered some telling observations about what he considered to be the proper role of partisan politics.

Disdaining the idea that "the two parties should represent opposed ideals and policies," Quigley insisted that "the two parties should be almost identical, so that the American people can 'throw the rascals out' at any election without leading to any profound or extensive shifts in policy." When the electorate grows weary of one of the Establishment parties, Quigley continued, "it should be able to replace it, every four years if necessary, by the other party, which ... will still pursue, with new vigor, approximately the same basic policies."[17]

The policies alluded to by Quigley — namely, incessant entanglement in foreign conflicts, and the relentless growth of socialism at home — constitute the much-heralded "bipartisan consensus." It is more accurately described as a pact between the parasites and plunderers — that is, the government and its favored constituencies — against the interests of the productive class.

Like Quigley, the late social critic Christopher Lasch documented the existence of this conspiratorial Power Elite, which he designated the "New Class." Unlike Quigley, however, Lasch condemned the Power Elite's machinations: "Those who control the international flow of money and information, preside over the philanthropic foundations and institutions of higher learning, manage the instruments of cultural production and thus set the terms of public debate ... have lost faith in the values, or what remains of them, of the West."[18]

Many of the most influential members of that elite, Lasch observed, "have ceased to think of themselves as Americans in any important sense, implicated in America's destiny for better or for worse." As a result, they are "deeply indifferent to the prospect of American decline." In fact, that elite heartily reviles "Middle America," a term which "has come to symbolize everything that stands in the way of progress": patriotism, religious devotion, strong family commitments, and conventional morality.[19]

Let's March!

Like the Mafia, the Power Elite commands tremendous wealth and power, yet its most formidable weapon remains *deception*. And, like the Mafia, its single greatest vulnerability is *exposure*.

Thus its designs can still be defeated if a sufficient number of Americans can be informed, organized, and mobilized — if, to paraphrase John Locke, we can "rouse [ourselves] and endeavor to put the rule into such hands which may secure ...

the ends for which government was at first erected...."

Most Americans, serene in the misplaced confidence that they live in the best of all possible worlds, don't realize three very important things:

- First, that their immediate ancestors — say, their parents and grandparents — enjoyed a higher standard of living than they do, measured in terms of what they owned, what they owed, and what they could transmit to their heirs.

- Second, that while the United States of America remains a "middle-class nation," it is tragically unlikely that it will remain so a generation from now, if it continues on its present course.

- Third, that this reflects the labors of a conspiratorial elite that can and must be defeated through organized, principled action.

What would happen if a sufficient number of Americans came to understand these three unsettling, but vital truths? We can see one possible outcome in the history of our struggle for independence.

Our Founders faced a predicament similar to ours. They had an extensive heritage of liberty, but confronted the daunting task of defeating a conspiracy against their liberties that had at its disposal the wealth and power of the world's most formidable empire. Yet our Founders — through courageous, principled, organized effort, and with God's help — prevailed in their struggle for independence, and succeeded in creating our constitutional republic. Because of their heroic labors, our task — unnerving though it may be — is much simpler: We have a constitutional framework that can still work, if Americans can be taught to use it correctly.

For nearly a half-century, The John Birch Society has done the vital work of exposing the Power Elite and its conspiratorial designs. The JBS has also led the way in educating the public about our heritage of limited government under law, and the role of an informed, mobilized electorate in reducing the size, scope, expense, and invasiveness of government.

Long before it became fashionable, the Society urged our nation to withdraw from the United Nations, the IMF, the World Bank, and other foreign entanglements. Today the JBS is leading the fight to prevent creation of the so-called Free Trade Area of the Americas — an EU-style regional government.

Creating the FTAA is perhaps the highest immediate priority of the criminal conspiracy that seeks to impoverish and enslave us. Defeating the FTAA should thus be the highest priority of those who cherish what its architects seek to destroy. And this is a struggle that we can win — if a sufficient number of Americans are informed and mobilized in time.

While defeating the FTAA is vital, it is not sufficient. We must also end our nation's entanglement in needless foreign conflicts, as well as our involvement in the UN and its affiliates; we must stop foreign aid, including the subsidized export of our manufacturing capacity abroad; we must restore control over our nation's borders. Just as importantly, our central government has to be trimmed back to proper constitutional size, so that our businesses are no longer being suffocated beneath regulations and bled dry by taxes.

The organized effort to destroy our civilization requires an organized opposition; when confronting combinations of bad men bent on total power, good people who love liberty must combine their efforts as well. The JBS has a proper understanding of the enemy, a winning strategy to defeat it, and the necessary organizational framework. The JBS program can succeed if enough Americans will enlist in this vital effort, while time remains.

Appendices

Appendices

Descent into Degeneracy

[Let us] create public schools where, as soon as they are weaned, the young may be reared; installed therein as ward of the State, the child can forget even his mother's name. After he has grown up, let him in turn couple indiscriminately, democratically, with his mates and brethren, doing as his parents did before him.

— The Marquis de Sade[1]

Satan is a word ... which represents rebellion, represents Man, represents a defiance toward society and God and the things that are forced upon us and are considered normal and acceptable.... There's a distinct lack of leadership, idols, icons and superstars for kids to identify with.... America needs that anti-Christ figure, that anti-hero to save these kids from the oppression of right wing morality.

— Transvestite "Goth Rocker" Marilyn Manson, self-described "minister" in the Church of Satan[2]

My only enemy is right-wing religious fundamentalism.

— U.S. President Bill Clinton[3]

For decades, Super Bowl Sunday has been an American middle-class institution. Whatever it may say about our priorities as a culture, the Super Bowl has become a secular holiday. Easily the most popular television spectacle, the game and its trappings provide a sense of national communion unmatched by any other event, attracting the eager eyes of tens of millions of Americans of all races, creeds, colors, and team loyalties.

This is what makes the event irresistible to advertisers, who pay extortionate rates to hawk their products to a global television audience. As the MTV-produced halftime show at the 2004 Super Bowl illustrated, the event is similarly irresistible to agents of cultural subversion. During the intermission of a tautly contested game, the New England Patriots and the Carolina Panthers surrendered the stage to what was appropriately described as a collection of "seemingly drugged, indifferent, writhing pagan figures."

"These [were] not living human beings in action," continued cultural critic Michael Novak, but rather "sacks of flesh, writhing, grinding, pawing, acting out no higher appeal than bodily functions.... A more radically anti-Jewish and anti-Christian assault, embodying the sort of Wagnerian images of pagan disgust and decadence that enraptured Hitlerian audiences, would be hard for them to produce."[4]

As if in conscious disdain for its middle-class audience, the producers of MTV's halftime spectacle organized an antic parade of filthy-mouthed "rappers" — borderline simian figures rhythmically chanting obscenities. The standout of this degenerate collection was Kid Rock, a talent-less, greasy-haired fleck of urban flotsam whose output (like most rap "music") is riddled with twelve-letter profanities. During the halftime show, Kid Rock celebrated America's favorite sporting event by garbing himself in a poncho fashioned from a desecrated American flag.

The halftime show's centerpiece featured Janet Jackson, clad in a sci-fi dominatrix getup, singing a duet with pop artist Justin Timberlake. Surrounding the singers was a troupe of dancers pantomiming sex acts. The song's refrain was an insistent promise that Timberlake would "get [Jackson] naked" by the number's end — a sentiment ultimately punctuated by Timberlake tearing off a portion of Jackson's wardrobe, exposing one of her breasts.

The incident had its intended effect, generating a media

furor eclipsing the game itself (a cliffhanger featuring several lead changes and a winning field goal with four seconds remaining) and provoking an FCC investigation. While the NFL indignantly denounced the MTV-produced halftime show, media critic Sally Jenkins pointed out that the league's protest over what she properly called "soft porn theater" was a little implausible.

"Exactly what did the league expect when it rented the MTV culture?" Jenkins asked. "What happened during the halftime show was that a bunch of leering, irreverent scream-voiced rock stars decided to make the NFL pay for its pretensions and profit-seeking.... [T]he point was obvious: Let's commandeer the audience of a hundred million for ourselves. And let's exploit their fun-for-the-whole-family-and-while-you're-at-it-buy-a-Ford-or-Cadillac sensibility.... The NFL tried to use MTV, and got used back."[5]

This is not to say that the degeneracy that tainted the 2004 Superbowl was limited to the halftime festivities. Many of the event's advertising spots "had an almost frat-house overtone that included bathroom humor," pointed out one review. "As usual, many of the biggest advertisers focused on making viewers yuk it up — but often with crude, lewd jokes. One year after a somewhat subdued Super Bowl atmosphere in which America was preparing for a war in Iraq, advertisers let loose with an R-rated comedy club for Super Bowl viewers."[6]

One of those responsible for choreographing this riotous festival of debauchery brazenly described the game plan. "It was a good mirror of what's going on in TV overall," commented Donny Deutsch, CEO of an advertising firm that created several of the Super Bowl ads. "Dumb is funny.... In many ways, it's a continuation of the dumbing down of America."[7]

For some, propagating stupidity is lucrative — at least for a while. But those with a more sober perspective understand that stupidity is not among the middle-class values — such as discipline, thrift, an appetite for self-improvement, self-sacrifice on behalf of one's posterity — that created our national prosperity. A debauched and dumbed-down culture is not one that will long remain prosperous and free.

But the truly ironic thing about the controversy triggered by Super Bowl XXXVIII's halftime show is this: Repellent though it was, it is entirely typical of the popular culture in which American youth are immersed. And the impact of that toxic culture can be felt in even respectable American communities.

Lost Children

Rockdale County, Georgia seemed to exemplify middle-class America. The Atlanta suburb played host to equestrian events during the 1996 Summer Olympics. The local economy was strong, the county school system was well-funded. Most residents of Conyers, the only town in the county, were materially comfortable and active in local churches. Thus it came as a shock when a syphilis outbreak occurred among Rockdale teenagers in the spring of 1996.[8]

Local health officials investigating the outbreak discovered behind Rockdale's middle-class façade a culture of predatory promiscuity rivaling — or even surpassing — that of the worst slums.

"It was not uncommon, when all the young people would get together, to engage in group sex," commented Professor Claire Sterk of the nearby Emory University School of Public Health, in the 1999 PBS *Frontline* documentary "The Lost Children of Rockdale County." "There was group sex going on in terms of one guy having sex with one of the girls, and then the next guy having sex with the same girl. There was group sex going on in terms of one girl having sex with multiple male partners at the same time, multiple females having sex with each other at the same time. I would say that the only type of group sex that I did not hear about in this overall context was group sex between just guys."[9]

Registered Nurse Cynthia Noel, who was among those who discovered the epidemic, referred to 14-year-old girls "with 20, 30, 40, 50 or 100 sex partners. You expect that of someone who is more into the line of being a prostitute or something." According to middle-school guidance counselor Peggy Cooper, the group sex incidents involved girls as young as 12 years old. "The parents were off and gone," observed Cooper. "And they said they were watching the Playboy Channel in the girl's bedroom. And there would be, like, 10 or 12 of them up there."[10]

One young boy told Cooper about the "game" their group had devised in which "you have to imitate what the Playboy people are doing." Another boy told her that "there may be three or four of us at one time. And it doesn't matter if you're two guys or two girls or a girl and a guy. It doesn't matter. You just have to do what they're doing."[11]

Another participant in the sex games recalled another party at which a young girl, equipped with "the bag of condoms we got from the health department," set out to have sex with every boy in the room. The boys at the party were "lined up ... it was like they were from the [bedroom] door to the front door.... And then she came out. She ... thought it was the coolest thing."[12]

The most horrifying segment of the program was an interview with three students identified as Katy, Bridget and Christine, who at the time were between 12 and 14 years of age. Like many of their friends, these waif-like girls were devoted fans of "hip-hop" and hardcore rap "music," a supposed art form produced by the gutter dregs of the inner city criminal subculture.

Liberal columnist Bob Herbert describes such "music" as the soundtrack of a " 'Lord of the Flies' street culture that is seducing one generation after another of black children, and producing freakish entertainers like Nelly and 50 Cent." Nelly (who was among the performers featured at Super Bowl

XXXVIII) is a "rapper" from St. Louis whose breakthrough hit was entitled "Pimp Juice." 50 Cent, the best-selling artist of 2003, hit the big-time with a ditty entitled "P.I.M.P.," another celebration of street prostitution.

The world inhabited by such alleged musicians is an inner-city hell-hole in which women are sexual playthings and males are willing to murder each other over any perceived offense. "We've got insane young men who take their heavy armament into the street and shoot up the neighborhood, and then go back inside to listen to music that celebrates the act of shooting up the neighborhood," laments Herbert.[13]

Katy, Bridget, and Christine lived in an almost entirely white, middle-class suburb, rather than an inner-city ghetto. But the Culture of Death, a full-service industry, delivers to the suburbs. Through MTV, those young girls became immersed in the "hip-hop" lifestyle. Prompted by the interviewer, the three girls — children — lapsed into something akin to a rhythmic trance while reciting the words to one of their favorite rap "songs" — an anatomically explicit celebration of group sex. "Is that something anybody does around here?" inquires the reporter. "Uh-huh! Lots of people. A lot of people," the girls replied.[14]

Just as shocking is the observation by one health worker that the girls who were involved in the Rockdale County orgies "were not homeless. They were not abused in any way. These were just normal, everyday, regular kids."[15] As if to underscore this point, the documentary described the goings-on at nearby Panama City, Florida, "a playground for teenagers from all over the country," according to the narration. "At the height of the season, thousands of high school students jam the two-lane highway and crowd the beaches, partying all night. Fights break out spontaneously and kids have sex in full view on the sand and on motel balconies overlooking the strip."

The wages of the perverse "freedom" enjoyed by Rockdale County youth were not limited to venereal disease. On May

20, 1999 — one month to the day after the hideous Columbine massacre — Conyers experienced its own school shooting.[16]

Cultivated Corruption

The experience of Rockdale County was shocking precisely because the community itself was so ordinary. Snugly ensconced in the Bible Belt, firmly entrenched in "Red State" America, Rockdale offered no haven from the dominant post-Christian culture. It was as if Mayberry had been transformed into Gomorrah.

Rockdale seemed to experience a harmonic convergence of troubling social trends: Overworked parents working up to 60 hours a week to retain a middle-class lifestyle; over-scheduled schoolchildren more passionately connected to their peers than to their families; an aggressively amoral school-based sex education system (typified by the bag of condoms toted by the young girl at the party mentioned above); and a deeply subversive, sex-saturated popular culture.

The "lost children" of Rockdale County are tragically typical of many American youth. This is not a reflection of cultural drift, but rather of a cultural hijacking. The lost youth didn't simply wander away; they have been carefully and deliberately misled as part of a scheme intended to capture our culture.

The late cultural commentator Richard Grenier observed that "capture the culture" was the battle cry of Italian Communist leader Antonio Gramsci. Consigned to prison by Mussolini (a one-time ally who imposed a different brand of militant collectivism on Italy), Gramsci "formulated in his *Prison Notebooks* the doctrine that those who want to change society must change man's consciousness, and that in order to accomplish this they must first control the institutions by which that consciousness is formed: schools, universities, churches, and, perhaps above all, art and the communications industry," recalled Grenier. "It is these institutions that shape and articulate 'public opinion,' the limits of which few politicians can violate with impunity. Culture, Gramsci felt, is not simply the superstructure of an economic base — the role assigned to it in orthodox Marxism — but is central to a society."[17]

Gramsci urged those who sought to bring about a "revolution in the state" to pursue the steady, incremental subversion of free societies by conducting a "long march through the institutions." In some ways the Gramscian approach is kindred to that pursued by Britain's Fabian socialists, who chose "patient gradualism," rather than violent insurrection, as the most effective means to collectivize society. Gramsci's distinctive insight was to urge Marxists to escape from the shackles of economic theory and focus instead on society's cultural organs — the press and other media, education, entertainment, religion, and the family. In order for revolutionaries to establish "political leadership or hegemony," advised Gramsci, they "must not count solely on the power and material force of government"; they must change the culture upon which that government was built.

Irredeemable Depravity

Many cultural commentators target the 1960s as the decade in which our Gramscian cultural revolution took hold. But the revolution actually occurred decades before its effects began to be noticed.

In his monumental 1966 study *Tragedy and Hope*, the late Georgetown University historian Carroll Quigley observed: "The period since 1950 has seen the beginnings of a revolutionary change in American politics. This change is not so closely related to changes in American economic life as it is to the transformation in social life.... What has been happening has been a disintegration of the middle class.... This disintegration of the middle classes had a variety of causes, some of them intrinsic, many of them accidental, a few of them obvious, but many of them going deeply into the very depths of social existence. All these causes acted to destroy the middle classes by acting to destroy the middle-class outlook." [18]

The chief "internal cause" of the "disintegration of the middle class" described by Quigley was not economic adversity, but rather the failure of that class "to transfer its outlook to its children … [a] failure [that] occurred chiefly within the middle-class family...." [19] The most important "external cause" was "the relentless attack [on middle-class values and institutions] in literature and drama throughout most of the twentieth century. In fact, it is difficult to find works that defended this outlook or even assumed it to be true, as was frequent in the nineteenth century." [20]

By mid-century, popular literature, drama, cinema, and the embryonic medium of television trafficked in "violence, social irresponsibility, sexual laxity and perversion … human weakness in relation to alcohol, narcotics, or sex.... The philosophic basis for this attack was found in an oversimplified Freudianism that regarded all suppression of human impulse as leading to frustration and psychic distortions that made subsequent life unattainable. Thus novel after novel or play after play portrayed the wickedness of the suppression of good, healthy, natural impulse and the salutary consequences of self-indulgence, especially in sex. Adultery and other manifestations of undisciplined sexuality were described in increasingly clinical detail...." [21]

The result of this "revolt against the middle class," Quigley pointed out, was "a total reversal of middle-class values by presenting as interesting or admirable simple negation of these values by aimless, shiftless, and totally irresponsible people." The entertainment industry was overwhelmed with "swamps of perversions ranging from homosexuality, incest, sadism … to cannibalism, necrophilia, and coprophagia." [22]

Bear in mind that Quigley wrote those words in the mid-1960s. That was an era when television censors wouldn't allow Barbara Eden, the buxom star of the sitcom "I Dream of

Jeanie," to display her navel; an era in which most local communities still had, and enforced, "blue laws," anti-obscenity ordinances, and other codes of public morality; it was a time prior to the 1969 Stonewall riot that inaugurated the homosexual revolution, and the 1973 *Roe vs. Wade* decision striking down state anti-abortion laws.

As one who had privileged access to the "papers and secret records" of the Power Elite, Quigley was describing not only what was taking place at the farthest fringes of radical culture, but also what the radicals and their Establishment mentors planned to inflict on our nation. (The chapter from which these observations are taken is entitled "The Future in Perspective.") The exponents of revolution denigrate the biblical view of man as a special creation of God placed "a little lower than the angels." As Quigley pointed out, the revolutionaries viewed man as "lower than any animal would naturally descend. From this has emerged the Puritan view of man (but without the Puritan view of God) as a creature of total depravity in a deterministic universe without hope of any redemption."[23]

To what end would this be done? Quigley pointed out that one strain of Puritanism was invoked in the 16th and 17th centuries (most notably in Thomas Hobbes' essay *Leviathan*) to justify despotism in the name of public order. The new doctrine of depravity "now may be used, with petty-bourgeois [lower and lower-middle-class] support, to justify a new despotism to preserve, by force instead of conviction, petty-bourgeois values in a system of compulsory conformity."[24]

In a self-governing society, public morality and private morality cannot be segregated. People who have abandoned what George Washington referred to as the "eternal rules of order and right" will be incapable of exercising the self-discipline necessary to maintain a free government.

In his *Farewell Address*, Washington advised that there is "no truth more thoroughly established than that there exists in the economy and course of nature an indissoluble union between virtue and happiness; between duty and advantage; between the genuine maxims of an honest and magnanimous policy and the solid rewards of public prosperity and felicity."

When such habits of virtue are cultivated and preserved, society can enjoy the blessings of limited government — one that will, in Jefferson's words, "restrain men from injuring one another, [and which] shall leave them otherwise free to regulate their own pursuits of industry and improvement, and shall not take from the mouth of labor the bread it has earned." Once those moral habits are discarded — or deliberately destroyed through subversion — the despotism of the Total State becomes the only alternative to anarchy.

And this is precisely the plan followed by Gramsci's disciples.

Elitist/Smut-peddler Axis

In an abortive investigation conducted in 1954, Tennessee Congressman Carroll Reece exposed significant elements of the Gramscian network laboring to destroy the American middle class. The Reece Committee probed the connections between tax-exempt foundations and various subversive organizations — most notably, the Council on Foreign Relations — working to bring about our nation's submergence in a global government. The inquiry also examined the work of left-leaning social scientists (such as Alfred Kinsey) and legal activists to destroy our country's moral foundations.

These cultural revolutionaries, warned Congressman Reece, sought to create a public culture in which "there are no absolutes, that everything is indeterminate, that no standards of conduct, morals, ethics, and government are to be deemed inviolate, that everything, including basic moral law, is subject to change, and that it is the part of the social scientists to take no principle for granted as a premise in social or juridical reasoning, however fundamental it may hereto have been deemed to be under our Judeo-Christian moral system." [25]

One of the most consequential beneficiaries of foundation funding (particularly from the Rockefellers) was Alfred C. Kinsey, lead author of the 1948 report *Sexual Behavior in the Human Male*. Former Kinsey Institute adviser James H. Jones, who knew Kinsey intimately, describes the renowned sexologist as a militant homosexual who sought to demolish America's conventional morality.[26]

Wardell Pomeroy, a close associate of Kinsey, recalled that "Kinsey knew a great deal about the Judeo-Christian tradition, and he was indignant about what it had done to our culture."[27] In their *Report on Male Sexuality*, Kinsey and his associates candidly expressed the view that "healthy" sexuality ignores all distinctions regarding "right and wrong, licit and illicit, normal and abnormal, acceptable and unacceptable...."[28]

The subjects used by Kinsey as a supposedly representative sample of American society were recruited from homosexual bars and culled from the ranks of sex offenders. In order to demonstrate that human beings are "sexual creatures" practically from birth, Kinsey and his comrades conducted ghastly experiments involving the "clinical" molestation of newborn infants.[29]

Among those who collaborated with Kinsey was Rene Guyon, a French Marxist and pederast who coined the saying, "sex by age eight or else it's too late." According to international sexologist Dr. Harry Benjamin (an associate of both Kinsey and Guyon), "Guyon developed a deconstructed legal theory [of sexual liberation], fortifying it with Kinsey's 'scientific' data. It was put into the hands of legal radicals like Morris Ernst, an advocate for the new sexual order, who handled revolutionary cases in his war against the American legal order."

To bring about the sexual revolution, nothing less than the utter demolition of the existing legal culture would suffice. In Ernst's 1948 book *American Sexual Behavior and the Kinsey Report*, Kinsey colleague Robert Dickinson claimed that "virtually every page of the Kinsey Report touches on some sec-tion of the legal code … a reminder that the law, like … our social pattern, falls lamentably short of being based on a knowledge of facts." Harmonizing American law with Kinsey's perverted vision of sexual emancipation became the mission of Ernst and his revolutionary associates.

Ernst was wired into the Gramscian network. He was affiliated with the American Civil Liberties Union (ACLU), the Sex Information and Education Council of the United States (SIECUS), and Planned Parenthood of America. He also enjoyed close ties to Supreme Court Justices Brandeis, Brennan, and Frankfurter, and Judge Learned Hand — all of whom were key judicial change agents in removing legal protections for conventional morality, the traditional family, and the sanctity of life.

Another of Kinsey's key legal allies was Professor Herbert Wechsler, a noted legal scholar at Columbia University, a one-time close confidant of President Franklin Roosevelt, and member of the National Lawyers Guild, a legal front for the Communist Party. Drawing on Kinsey's "research," Wechsler composed a Model Penal Code for the American Legal Institute (ALI), a Rockefeller- and Carnegie-subsidized educational arm of the American Bar Association. The key element of that model statute — what lawyers would call the "gravamen" — is that there should be no "criminal penalties for consensual sexual relations conducted in private."

The next year, the ALI Model Penal Code was immediately touted as a model to state legislatures. Ernst urged his Gramscian comrades to "establish a Committee on the Laws of Sexual Behavior and consider their own State's legal system in this field…." In short order, those committees were established with funding from the Rockefeller Foundation, and — using the Model Penal Code as their model — those committees began working for new laws that either eliminated or trivialized sex crimes, from homosexuality to public indecency.

At the same time, Ernst's comrades in the federal court system — including allies on the Supreme Court — carried out a flanking attack against states and communities that didn't toe the ALI line. In a string of decisions dealing with contraception (*Griswold v. Connecticut*, 1965; *Eisenstadt v. Baird*, 1972; *Carey v. Population Services International*, 1977), pornography (*Miller v. California*, 1973), and abortion (*Roe v. Wade* and *Doe v. Bolton*, 1973), the Supreme Court usurped the state governments' reserved powers to set social policies regarding moral issues.

For many of the Libertarian or libertine persuasion, these developments were a welcome emancipation of the individual from onerous laws regulating moral conduct. But the crusade to liberate the libido had contributed greatly to the demolition of the constitutional powers reserved to states and local communities, while simultaneously enhancing the powers of the central government. And the horrifying experience of Rockdale County — as well as thousands of other communities — illustrates that the sexual revolution has entered its own reign of terror.

"Social Marketing" of Porn

For Rockdale County's lost children, pornography — specifically the Playboy Channel — offered detailed tutorials in sexual degeneracy. This is entirely in keeping with the purpose of modern pornography: Rather than simply catering to prurient interests, porn carries out a revolutionary function.

Speaking in the 1980s, Hugh Hefner — the founder of the Playboy empire — boasted: "The generation now running society is the first Playboy generation."[30] *Playboy* and its descendants have done more than any other institution, judicial ruling, or media organ to propagate Kinsey's gospel of post-Christian sexual emancipation.

Dr. Judith Reisman elaborates on the grim reality behind Hefner's triumph:

[T]his is largely a Playboy-reared society as well. And it is a Kinsey-reared society as well. Hefner and Kinsey share the responsibility for a generation of heterophobia — fear and distrust of the opposite sex — wide-spread drug use and addiction, impotence and homosexuality, suicide, astronomical divorce rates, epidemics of venereal disease, and AIDS.... Both Kinsey and Hefner battled for the elimination and liberalization of sex laws.... Eventually tens of thousands of criminals, primarily sex offenders, were paroled back into society.... The measure of success for Kinsey and Hefner can be seen everywhere. Post Kinsey/Hefner, the profession of 'sexology' was created to cope with a massive increase in cases of sexual disorders. Building on its fraudulent research base, sexology crept into higher education, medicine, counseling, therapy, law and public policy, sex and AIDS education, curricula, and political lobbying.[31]

Hefner's empire created a tax-exempt foundation to re-invest a portion of its extravagant profits in funding subversive "research."[32] "*Playboy* is one of the most important magazines in the world, in terms of the impact it's had not only on social mores but as a champion of individual rights," boasted Hef--ner in 1974. "We've supported countless civil liberties organizations, political reform, sex research and education, abortion reform before it became popular, prison reform, and the continuing campaign to reform our repressive sex and drug laws …"[33]

Indeed, following the Supreme Court's 1973 *Roe v. Wade* decision abolishing state laws protecting unborn human beings from abortion, *Playboy* conspicuously cut itself in for a share of the credit. "The Playboy Foundation participated in a movement that won a major court victory," crowed the magazine's January 1974 issue. "The victory came with last January's Supreme Court decision legalizing abortion. This was especially gratifying because of the Foundation's long campaign for reform, which began in 1966."[34]

Incredible as it may seem, Hefner and his creation have actually been embraced by some self-styled conservatives. William F. Buckley Jr., the media-designated leader of American conservatism, has been a frequent contributor to the pages of Hefner's smut sheet. *National Review*, Buckley's magazine, ran not one but two laudatory pieces marking the 50th anniversary of Hefner's porn empire.[35] One of them insisted that "*Playboy* really does have something to do with freedom, and these days maybe that's worth remembering. A society that allows *Playboy* is not a society that allows women to be stoned to death for adultery."[36]

Indeed not: On the basis of our national experience we can safely say that a society that allows *Playboy* will — within the course of a generation — embrace legalized and subsidized child-killing and repeal many of the laws intended to protect women from sexual violence.

Godfather of the Smut Industry

But Hefner has long been eclipsed — both as a porn kingpin and "social activist" — by Harvard-educated Philip Harvey, the so-called "Godfather" of the porn industry.

From his redoubt in Hillsborough, North Carolina, Harvey operates PHE, Inc. — the nation's largest distributor of hardcore porn videos and other sex-related products. Like Mafia chieftains trekking to New York City to confer with the "Commission" heading La Cosa Nostra, the leading producers of smut films regularly travel to Hillsborough in search of financing and project approval.[37]

Harvey himself regularly treks to Washington, D.C., to supervise Population Services International, a nonprofit corporation that works closely with the federal government and international organizations to promote population control overseas. To Harvey, peddling porn and promoting an anti-natal agenda are part of the same mission, which he describes as "social marketing" — applying "the power and creativity of the private sector to family planning." In 1969, as a graduate student at the University of North Carolina-Chapel Hill, Harvey received a grant from the Ford Foundation (a major underwriter of cultural subversion) to do graduate work on "family planning." His graduate thesis was a proposal for mail-order marketing of condoms — a revolutionary idea that essentially served as a business proposal for PHE, Inc.[38]

For its first few years, Harvey's mail-order business floundered. His fortunes turned around, however, when he began to include erotic photographs in his catalog. In 1975, Harvey introduced the "Adam & Eve" catalog, which marketed sex aids and hard-core pornography along with "socially responsible" contraceptives. Most importantly, Harvey's mail-order business (which Supreme Court rulings made possible by overturning laws against interstate commerce in pornography) gave porn consumers anonymity and privacy. They no longer had to skulk about in dingy neighborhoods, casting around furtive glances in fear of being recognized. Thirty million copies of the "Adam & Eve" catalog are distributed each year, attracting more than two million paying customers. All of PHE's products are vetted by consultants from an august-sounding group called the American Association of Sex Educators, Counselors, and Therapists.[39]

Harvey's fortune, built one "plain brown wrapper" at a time, put him in the interesting position of being simultaneously pursued and courted by the federal government. "During the late 1980s, while officials at the Justice Department were doing all they could to put Harvey in prison for obscenity violations, officials at the State Department's Agency for International Development were working closely with him to make contraceptives widely available in the Third World," observes investigative author Eric Schlosser.[40]

The federal crackdown on the porn industry during the Reagan and Bush I administrations "wiped out many of [Harvey's] mail-order competitors and dissuaded others from entering the business" — thereby giving the Ford-funded Establishment pornographer what amounts to a federally protected concession. And while Harvey continues to rake in money from his mail-order skin trade, he "still travels regularly to developing nations to meet with the administrators of his family planning projects," notes Schlosser.

While the alliance between America's porn "Godfather" and the international population control movement may strike some as ironic, it's actually entirely appropriate: All of these people view the conventional American middle class family as the enemy. Breaking down America's middle-class — and preventing other societies from adopting it as a model — is their shared objective.

In 1967, British population control activist Kingsley Davis pointed out that the social factors relevant to reducing the growth of the human population are "beyond the control of family planning ... the social structure and economy must be changed before a deliberate reduction in the birthrate can be achieved.... Changes basic enough to affect motivation for having children would be changes in the structure of the family, in the position of women and in the sexual mores."[41]

Two years later, Frederic Jaffe, president of Planned Parenthood, elaborated on Davis's recommendations in a memorandum to Bernard Berelson, president of the Population Council. (The Population Council was created by David Rockefeller as a means of coordinating international population control efforts.)

The Berelson Memorandum, which was published in the October 1970 issue of *Family Planning Perspectives*, listed four categories of population control options: "Social Constraints," "Economic Deterrents/Incentives," "Social Controls," and "Housing Policies." Among the "Social Constraints" discussed in this population control blueprint could be found "compulsory education of children," the encouragement of "increased homosexuality," as well as propaganda and social engineering efforts to alter the "image of the ideal family." Other draconian measures contemplated in that memo included placement of "fertility control agents in [the] water supply," "compulsory abortion of out-of-wedlock pregnancies," sterilization of couples following their second child, and the issuance of government "permits" to couples as a condition of having children.[42]

Clear-cutting Society

"For more than five centuries," writes *Atlantic Monthly* investigative reporter Eric Schlosser in his new book *Reefer Madness*, "radical social movements [have] embraced pornography." From Renaissance-era humanists, to the leaders of the 18th-century "Enlightenment" (including the notorious Marquis de Sade), to the exponents of the San Francisco-based 1960s counterculture, pornography has been used to bring about "a profound shift in public attitudes toward sex, as religious influences gave way to secular ones."[43] In the case of 21st Century America, that shift has been accomplished with astonishing speed.

In the January 1996 issue of the Marxist journal *Dissent*, Michael Walzer took stock of the victories won by the radical left in the Culture War — which he tellingly described as "the Gramscian war of position."[44] Among the triumphs Walzer listed were:

- "The emergence of gay rights politics, and … the attention paid to it in the media";
- "The transformation of family life: the first successful challenge to male authority and the traditional division of labor [within the home] … rising divorce rates, changing sexual mores, new household arrangements — and, again, the portrayal of all this in the media";
- "The progress of secularization; the fading of religion in

general and Christianity in particular from the public
sphere — classrooms, textbooks, legal codes, holidays,
and so on";
• "The legalization of abortion."[45]

What Walzer describes is the clear-cutting of all social institutions — beginning with the middle-class family — that
impede the creation of the Total State.

Again, many might find it difficult to believe that radical
sexual emancipation can co-exist with severe political regi-
mentation. But this approach was used quite successfully by
the architects of Sweden's all-encompassing socialist welfare
state. " 'Freedom' in Swedish is a word that appears to be
taboo," observed British journalist Roland Huntford in his
1971 book *The New Totalitarians*, a critical study of Sweden's
version of cradle-to-grave collectivism. "There is one excep-
tion, however, and that is in sexual matters. In the same way
that 'security' is the creed of [Swedish socialist] politics, so is
'liberty' that of sex."[46]

This connection between sexual license and political tyranny was described by Aldous Huxley in the preface to the 1948
edition of his masterpiece *Brave New World*:

> As political and economic freedom diminishes, sexual
> freedom tends compensatingly to increase. And the dic-
> tator (unless he needs cannon fodder and families with
> which to colonize empty or conquered territories) will
> do well to encourage that freedom. In conjunction with
> the freedom to daydream under the influence of dope,
> the movies and the radio, [sexual emancipation] will
> help to reconcile his subjects to the servitude which is
> their fate.

The Wages of Perpetual War

Of all the enemies to public liberty, war is, perhaps, the most to be dreaded, because it comprises and develops the germ of every other. War is the parent of armies; from these proceed debts and taxes; and armies, and debts, and taxes are the known instruments for bringing the many under the domination of the few.... No nation could preserve its freedom in the midst of continual warfare.
— James Madison, 1795

We are not going to achieve a new world order without paying for it in blood as well as in words and money.
— Historian Arthur Schlesinger Jr.[1]

We shouldn't have been there in the first place.... We have people in America who don't have health care benefits, and they're sending health care benefits to Iraqis? America's in the role of global policeman, and we're going to fill that role until it destroys us.
— Justin Madeiros, teenage son of an Army reservist deployed to Iraq on "peacekeeping" duty[2]

We've got the best recruiting force in the world. We've got a soft economy, and we've got opportunities that resonate with young Americans.
— Col. Thomas Nickerson, director of strategic outreach for the U.S. Army Accessions Command[3]

War is an unfortunate reality of the human condition, one that will plague us for the foreseeable future. For those whose views are shaped by the Western "Just War" tradition, there are only a handful of cases in which war is justified. In fact, where war is permissible, it is essentially mandatory: No moral man can refuse to fight when necessary to protect the innocent and defend freedom.

The Armed Forces of the United States have a noble and honorable legacy. They also have the distinction of being the first fighting force in human history created for the exclusive purpose of upholding the principles of republican liberty enshrined in a written constitution. Our independence and liberty depend, to a large extent, on the willingness of Americans to enlist for service under our nation's flag.

The American Founding Fathers, who had wrested their independence from Great Britain by trial of arms, understood the necessity of providing for a strong defense. They also understood, and moved to pre-empt, the danger posed by standing military establishments, which historically have been perverted into instruments of tyranny.[4] The Founders understood that where war is necessary to protect our liberties and independence, it must be fought, won — *and ended*. As Madison warned, neither liberty nor prosperity can survive a state of perpetual war.

Gateway to Perpetual War

In the wake of 9-11, most Americans understood that a military response of some type, against some foreign enemy, was inevitable. Of course, more than a few wondered why, in light of the hundreds of billions of dollars spent each year on "defense," our federal government was unable to prevent the lethal terrorist strike against our most prominent cities by 19 knife-wielding fanatics. But most of those critics understood that an act of war had been committed against our country, one that demanded a military reply — assuming, of course, that the enemy could be identified.

President George W. Bush quickly identified notorious terrorist chieftain Osama bin Laden, who at the time was residing in Afghanistan, as the mastermind of the Black Tuesday atrocity. Had President Bush asked for a declaration of war against Afghanistan, he almost certainly would have received one from Congress. But Congress chose instead to issue an open-ended resolution approving the use of force against any nation or foreign power the president adjudged to be in league with terrorists. This resolution — along with various UN Security Council resolutions — was used to justify the invasion and occupation of Afghanistan.[5]

A similar formula was followed when, in March 2003, the Bush administration invaded and occupied Iraq: Again, the president invoked various UN Security Council resolutions and a congressional resolution supposedly authorizing the president to enforce them.[6]

The Bush administration insisted that Iraq posed an immediate threat to our nation. By the end of 2003, it was clear that it never did — a conclusion confirmed beyond dispute by the congressional testimony of chief U.S. arms inspector David Kay in early 2004. Shortly before the war began, a national opinion poll revealed that a majority of the American public believed that Saddam Hussein had been involved in the 9-11 attacks. By late 2003, however, administration officials from the president on down admitted that it had no evidence of an Iraqi role in 9-11, or of significant ties with the al-Qaeda terrorist network blamed for the atrocity.

Immediately before the war began, the administration abruptly changed the party line again: Now the war was to serve the humane purpose of liberating Iraqis from the grip of the despotic Saddam Hussein — a tyrant whose regime had prospered as a client of both Washington and Moscow.[7] Practically on the eve of the war, President Bush made a public address in which he described the impending conflict as the opening phase of a regional "democratic" revolution in the Middle East — a concept that he eventually expanded into a global "democratic revolution."[8]

In a November 2003 speech in London's Whitehall Palace, Mr. Bush insisted that "we now have only two options [in Iraq]: to keep our word, or to break our word. The failure of democracy in Iraq would throw its people back into misery and turn that country over to terrorists who wish to destroy us. Yet democracy will succeed in Iraq, because our will is firm, our word is good, and the Iraqi people will not surrender their freedom." Keeping our "word," he explained, would also mean paying additional billions of dollars in foreign aid, intervening elsewhere in order to promote the global "democratic revolution," and working to bolster the credibility of the United Nations as "an effective instrument of our collective security.... [T]he credibility of the UN depends on a willingness to keep its word and to act when action is required."

Indeed, admitted Mr. Bush, the chief purpose of the war in Iraq is to "prevent the United Nations from solemnly choosing its own irrelevance and inviting the fate of the League of Nations." This was the central point of the president's address — which was captured in the headline chosen for the *London Guardian*'s story about the speech: "Iraq war saved the UN, says president."

War for the "Core"

The Iraq war left the United States with roughly half of our military entrenched in the Middle East. According to Thomas P.M. Barnett, a Pentagon "futurist" and key adviser to Defense Secretary Donald Rumsfeld, entangling our military in the region is actually the most important achievement of the war.

"When the United States finally goes to war again in the Persian Gulf," wrote Barnett shortly before the war began, "it will not constitute a settling of old scores, or just an enforced disarmament of illegal weapons, or a distraction in the war on terror. Our next war in the Gulf will mark a historical tipping point — the moment when Washington takes real ownership of strategic security in the age of globalization. This is why the public debate about this war has been so important: It forces Americans to come to terms with … the new security paradigm that shapes this age, namely, *Disconnectedness defines danger*. Saddam Hussein's outlaw regime is dangerously disconnected from the globalizing world, from its rule sets, its norms, and all the ties that bind countries together in mutually assured dependence."[9]

In the aftermath of 9-11, Barnett, a professor of warfare analysis at the U.S. Naval War College, repeatedly offered a standard briefing to high-level military officials and policymakers at the Pentagon. That briefing focused on a division of the world between the "Functioning Core" — nations that had been assimilated into the global system of "collective security" and managed trade — and the "Non-Integrating Gap" — nations yet to be assimilated. A small number of nations were designated "seam states" along the border between the Core and the Gap.

The operative security principle in the global age, pontificated Barnett, is: "*A country's potential to warrant a U.S. military response is inversely related to its globalization connectivity*.... If we step back for a minute and consider the broader implications of this new global map, then U.S. national-security strategy would seem to be: 1) Increase the Core's immune system capabilities for responding to September 11-type perturbations; 2) Work the seam states to firewall the Core from the Gap's worst exports, such as terror, drugs, and pandemics; and, most important, 3) *Shrink the Gap*."[10]

Where does the war on Iraq fit into this picture? Barnett offered a revealing answer: "The real reason I support a war like this is that the resulting long-term military commitment will finally force America to deal with the entire Gap as a strategic threat environment."[11] The "Gap," it should be explained, is everything outside of "North America, much of South America, the European Union, Putin's Russia, Japan and Asia's emerging economies (most notably China and India), Australia and New Zealand, and South Africa...." Taken together, "Gap" and "Seam" states account for roughly two billion people, including hundreds of millions of unemployed or under-employed Third World young men — potential recruits for terrorist or guerrilla movements.[12]

Tellingly, the single most important criterion for membership in the "Core," according to Barnett, is a nation's membership in the World Trade Organization (WTO). Citing the example of Communist China, a nation designated a member of the "Core" despite being ruled by "a 'Communist party' whose ideological formula is 30 percent Marxist-Leninist and 70 percent *Sopranos*," Barnett explains that WTO membership forces each member state "to harmonize its internal rule set with that of globalization — banking, tariffs, copyright protection, environmental standards.... Trying to adapt to globalization does not mean that bad things will never happen to you. Nor does it mean all your poor will immediately morph into stable middle class.... [I]t is always possible to fall off this bandwagon called globalization. And when you do, bloodshed will follow. If you are lucky, so will American troops."[13]

Most Americans would object to the notion that America's military is intended to be a global constabulary force, rather than to defend our homeland and its citizens. But as Barnett approvingly observes, since the supposed "end of the Cold War," the U.S. military has been used exclusively as globocops. Between 1990 and 2002, the U.S. military was dispatched on 132 separate foreign deployments — wars, major air campaigns, occupations, and so on — all of which involved "countries having trouble with globalization.... The disconnected countries are where you'll find instability. That's where you'll find threats to the international system and the global economy."[14]

Rather than protecting our nation and its Constitution from "all enemies, foreign and domestic," under the emerging globalist vision the U.S. military's job is forcibly to assimilate nations into the centrally managed "global economy." Rather than fighting and dying on behalf of home and hearth, American servicemen are now expected to kill and die on behalf of the UN, the WTO, and the other instruments of global "connectivity." And American civilians are expected to sacrifice on behalf of "connectivity" as well:

> In an increasingly smaller world, we will be living with violence and terror unless we open up the world's bad neighborhoods to economic opportunity. We have to fight those who would hijack societies and disconnect them from the global economy. We have to accept some emigrants from aspiring countries. But more important, we need to accept their imports and help them get on a sensible development path.[15]

It's all quite simple, according to Barnett. Our tax dollars, industrial capacity, and servicemen will be sent abroad in the interest of building the global economy; developing nations will send us wave after wave of low-priced imports as well as their unemployable emigrants.

As historian Arthur Schlesinger Jr. observed nearly a decade ago, "We are not going to achieve a new world order without paying for it in blood as well as in words and money."[16] The toll inflicted on our nation by the war in Iraq is merely a down payment on the price of building the connected world envisioned by the Power Elite, and described in such clinical fashion by Barnett. To those whose sons, daughters, fathers, and mothers return from Iraq in shipping tubes, that price is much too high.

Demolishing Saddam's ruling infrastructure was relatively easy; restoring some semblance of order afterwards proved to be a much larger challenge. Scores of Americans died in the initial invasion. Hundreds more were killed by guerrilla attacks after May 1, 2003, the day President George W. Bush claimed that "major military operations" in Iraq were over. Thousands of others were wounded, many of them left incapacitated by combat wounds or illness.

By the end of November 2003, the total number of American casualties in Iraq — killed in action, wounded, injured, or gravely ill — had reached 9,675, the numerical equivalent of nearly a full Army division.[17] "I don't think even that is the whole story," contended Nancy Lessin of Boston, whose son fought in Iraq. "We think there's an effort to hide the true cost in life, limb and the mental health of our soldiers. There's a larger picture here of really trying to hide and obfuscate what's going on, and the wounded and injured are part of it."[18]

Not included in that grim compilation are the homefront casualties — such as families left in grim economic circumstances as their breadwinners are deployed abroad.

Those Who Bear the Burden

As a young man, Mike Gorski of Hayward, California served four years in the United States Marines. After mustering out of the Corps, Gorski enlisted in the National Guard — one weekend of training a month, two weeks on active duty. He then married, started a family, and began a career as a banker.

Gorski and tens of thousands of other Guardsmen and Army Reservists were called to active duty following the terrorist attack of September 11, 2001. And like hundreds of thousands of Americans in uniform, Gorski was deployed to Iraq after the March 2003 invasion of that country — which was sold to the public as necessary to pre-empt a possible Iraqi terrorist strike on our homeland.

Mike Gorski's unit, the 870th Military Police Company of the California National Guard, included "teachers, bankers, mortgage brokers, telecommunications experts, police officers, and copy machine repairmen," reported the *New York Times*. "There is a father who has not seen his first child, one who has not seen his second and a grandfather who is raising his grandson." [19]

These part-time soldiers were told that their tour would last six months. As the morass deepened in Iraq, their deployment was eventually expanded to a full year — a development that prompted widespread protests from Guard and Reserve families. "You can't rely on these occupations … to be done by the Guard and Reserves," observed Florida Senator Bill Nelson. "They have a specialized niche, and in times of war, that's one thing. But in times of long, lengthy occupations, you can't take them away from their employers [and their families]." [20]

Employers of Guardsmen and Reservists are required by law to hold their jobs for them while the servicemen are deployed abroad. However, they are not required — and should not be expected — to keep paying salaries to their absent employees. Fortunately for Gorski's family, his patriotic employer continued to pay his salary, permitting his wife to make mortgage payments and to assume a volunteer role leading a support group for other families of the 870th. Within a few months Mrs. Gorski had run up an $11,000 credit card bill from phone calls, postage costs, care packages, and paying for family support meetings and dinners. But many of the families Mrs. Gorski tended to were in much worse financial condition.

Specialist Jory Preston, a telecommunications worker from Pleasant Hill, California, enlisted with the National Guard in January 2003 as a way to make ends meet. He and his wife married in February; a month later, with his wife expecting their first child, Jory was en route to Iraq. Preston's employer chose to stop paying his salary. As a result, his family — his wife and newborn child — lost $2,000 a month. After giving birth, Jory's wife Anita was forced to move out of the couple's apartment and move in with her father. She also succumbed to clinical depression.

"They told us when we first got deployed it would be six months — the whole thing," stated Preston. "I thought I could handle that. I wasn't aware of my wife's situation and I thought

I could suck it up and drive on, as the soldiers say."[21]

"Right now, it's the small things that play on the minds of the families left behind," stated Jeanean McKiever, who organized a support group called A Family of One for spouses and children of Reservists deployed to Iraq. Apart from obvious concerns over mortgage payments, medical bills, and other large expenses, families suddenly deprived of up to half of the expected household income must deal with smaller expenses that are usually taken for granted. "What about the [Thanksgiving] turkey? How can we afford school supplies?"

Compounding the financial hardships suffered by families of Guardsmen was what Congressman Christopher Shays called "a virtual systemic meltdown" of the military pay system: An incredible 94 percent of mobilized National Guardsmen experienced problems receiving their pay. According to a Guardsman who served as paymaster for a unit in Afghanistan, every soldier in his company had "some form of pay problem." One waited six weeks to get his first check; another had his wages improperly garnished for four months. Another spent each week making cost-prohibitive satellite telephone calls home "trying to determine if he's been paid correctly and making sure his family [had] enough money to pay the bills."[22]

Those Left Behind

The emotional toll of prolonged deployment, although impossible to tabulate objectively, is just as formidable as the financial burden. "Do these women miss their men? Believe me, they face that emotional change from the day he packs his bag and leaves," observed Jeanean McKiever, who was born and raised in a military family. "Can they stay faithful for a whole year? I'm not even going there but I'll tell you that there is going to be a big problem when the men do get home."

Lengthy deployments abroad can result in other domestic complications. When Army Reservist Jamie Peters was deployed to Iraq in February 2003, his daughter Laila was five months old. For months afterward, she would smile and exclaim "Dada!" whenever she saw a picture of her father. By the time she was a year old, however, her typical reaction had changed: She would throw the picture down and cry, "No!"[23]

Guardsman Eric Kinslow of Brookings, South Dakota, was in Iraq when his son Toby was born. Had his wife not been seven months pregnant, she would have been sent to Iraq as well when her Guard unit was called up.[24] The Kinslows were hardly the only two-soldier family affected by the war. Sgt. First Class Vaughn and Specialist Simone Holcomb of Colorado Springs were both called up for service in Iraq, leaving behind seven children in the care of Vaughn's mother and ex-wife.[25]

Simone had served in the National Guard before joining the Army. "In an ideal world, I wanted to be a soldier and a mom," she recalled. It's also safe to assume that raising a family of seven children required more income than Vaughn could provide alone. However, after the couple was called to serve their country abroad, Vaughn's ex-wife filed for custody of the three daughters they had prior to the divorce.

After Vaughn and Simone were granted an emergency leave to contest the claim, a judge ruled that one of them must remain behind to care for the children. It was decided that Vaughn would return to his tank platoon, and Simone — defying an order to return to Iraq — chose to remain behind. She was given an administrative punishment and threatened with criminal charges for going AWOL. Eventually Simone was taken off active duty and quietly returned to the Guard without further punishment.[26]

As the Iraq conflict deepened, commentator Bill Kauffman described the increasingly common spectacle of "women reservists, young mothers of infants and small children, leaving their families to go halfway 'round the world to act as cogs, expendable parts, in the machinery of the … Empire."[27] One

of them was Lori Piestewa, the Hopi woman from Arizona —
and mother of two small children — killed in the attack that
wounded Jessica Lynch.

Widespread disruption of family life is an inevitable by-
product of long-term foreign conflict. Notes Kauffman: "The
Second World War, by removing men from households and removing many of those households from the rural South into
the unwelcoming urban North, waged its own mini-war upon
the American family. Rosie the Riveter propaganda aside, the
domestic face of the warfare state was sketched by an Arkansas
social worker: 'Children's fathers go off to war and their mothers go to work, and thus the interests of parents is diverted from
the home and the children.' "[28]

One significant difference between World War II and the
open-ended "war on terrorism" is that too frequently both the
father *and* the mother are sent off to war.

Not surprisingly, all of these problems have led to collaps-
ing morale and severe attrition in terms of recruitment and retention of Guardsmen and Reservists. "Retention is what I am
most worried about," admitted Lt. General James Helmly, head
of the Army Reserve. "This is the first extended-duration war
the country has fought with an all-volunteer force." Although
historically the Guard and Reserve were designed to be deployed rapidly and then brought home immediately, they have
now entered what Lt. Gen. Helmly calls a "brave new world"
of lengthy, dangerous deployments abroad. This could result
in Reservists being deployed for 15 months or more at a
stretch.[29]

The National Guard was originally intended to serve as
each state's "select militia." In the post-September 11 environment, however, both the regular Army and the National
Guard are being transformed into a "nation-building force"
ready for rapid deployment anywhere in the world on short
notice. And foreign deployments of a year or more will "likely become the norm."[30] This assumes, of course, that the

Guard and Reserves will be able to attract and keep skilled personnel.

"People are dropping out left and right," commented an officer in the Army Reserve from Milwaukee. National Guard Association spokesman John Goheen admitted that "there is some concern over current operations tempo.... How much is too much? How much will it impact recruiting?"[31]

Perpetual War vs. Prosperity

As James Madison warned, liberty and prosperity cannot long endure "in the midst of continual warfare." War is the single greatest stimulant to government growth; it devours wealth, destroys capital, sows lasting enmities, and deprives society of its bravest and most capable men. It is occasionally a necessary evil, but it is no less evil when it proves to be necessary. Even when fought for the right reasons, war is a plague. When inflicted on a population for the wrong reasons, it is a singular crime.

In order to create the centrally directed global economy described by Barnett, our nation must assume the sorrowful burdens of empire until — deprived of our liberties, stripped of our prosperity, and bloodied by endless foreign conflicts — our depleted nation surrenders its independence to the global government our rulers are assembling even now.

Endnotes

CHAPTER ONE — Race to the Bottom

1. Taylor Caldwell, "Saving the Middle Class," *The New American*, June 23, 1997, p. 39.
2. "As Factory Jobs Disappear, Workers Have Few Options," *New York Times*, September 13, 2003.
3. "Free Trade's Victims Turning Against Bush, GOP," Durham *Herald-Sun*, August 25, 2003.
4. Jerry Skoff, interview with author.
5. "A North Carolina Town, Unraveled," *Washington Post*, August 9, 2003, p. E01.
6. "Booming China Trade Rankles U.S.," *Christian Science Monitor*, August 5, 2003.
7. Ibid.
8. "Brokers, developers, investors studying assets for sale," *Charlotte Observer*, August 7, 2003.
9. "Laid-Off Factory Workers Find Jobs Are Drying Up For Good," *Wall Street Journal*, July 21, 2003.
10. " 'Jobs, Jobs, Jobs' Mantra Returns to Haunt GOP," *CQ Weekly*, September 13, 2003.
11. "President's Remarks on Labor Day," official White House transcript, September 1, 2003.
12. John Crudele, "How the Government Is Using a Shell Game to Fool You," *New York Post*, September 9, 2003.
13. Ibid.
14. "Pulling the Plug: Factory Jobs Drift Abroad to Keep U.S. Company Afloat," ABC News, August 14, 2003.
15. Ibid.
16. Ibid.
17. Ibid.
18. Ibid.
19. Ibid.
20. Skoff.
21. John C. McCoy, interview with author.

22. *Christian Science Monitor*.

23. Skoff.

24. *Report to Congress*, Executive Summary, U.S.-China Security Review Commission and the U.S. Trade Deficit Review Commission, July 2002.

25. "Visclosky and Bayh still working to prevent move of Magnequench to China," *Chesterton Tribune*, August 6, 2003.

26. "Erosion of U.S. Industrial Base Is Troubling," *National Defense*, August 2003.

27. Pat Choate and Edward Miller, "An Analysis: The US Industrial Base and China"; accessed at http://www.uscc.gov/analysis.htm on September 23, 2003.

28. Ibid.

29. Ben Worthen, "No Americans Need Apply," *CIO Magazine*, September 2003.

30. Ibid.

31. Ibid.

32. William F. Jasper, "Your Job May Be Next!" *The New American*, March 10, 2003.

33. "Where the Good Jobs Are Going," *Time*, July 28, 2003.

34. "White-collar jobs moving abroad," *Christian Science Monitor*, July 29, 2003.

35. Louis T. March and Brent Nelson, *The Great Betrayal: The Elite's War on Middle America* (Raleigh, N.C.: Representative Government Press, 1995), pp. 11-12.

36. "Middle Class Barely Treads Water," *USA Today*, September 14, 2003.

37. Ibid.

38. Kurt Richebacher, "The Last Analysis"; accessed at http://www.gold-eagle.com/gold_digest_03/richebacher071103 pv.html on September 15, 2003.

39. Robert Morrow, "Living in the Bubble," *American Conservative*, February 10, 2003.

40. Ibid.

41. "More fall behind on mortgage: Foreclosures may rise if job

losses continue," *San Francisco Chronicle*, Sept. 11, 2003.

42. Morrow.

43. "Asia fills her boots: dollar reserves skyrocket," *Asia Times*, July 15, 2003.

44. Morrow.

CHAPTER TWO — Banishing Businesses

1. Quoted in Fred Smith, "The Thin Green Line," *Liberty*, January 2004, p. 16.

2. "Jon Huntsman slams energy policies," *Deseret Morning News*, September 8, 2003.

3. William L. Shirer, *The Rise and Fall of the Third Reich: A History of Nazi Germany* (New York: Simon & Schuster, 1960), p. 262.

4. "A Nation of Lawbreakers?" *Wall Street Journal*, March 12, 1993, page 1-A.

5. "Briggs & Stratton jobs could move overseas," *Milwaukee Journal-Sentinel*, September 8, 2003.

6. Ibid.

7. "Briggs warns of 22,000 lost jobs," *Milwaukee Journal-Sentinel*, September 16, 2003.

8. "Extreme CA Emissions Proposal Would Cost Heartland 22,000 Manufacturing Jobs; Small Engine Maker Could Be Forced Overseas, Study Examines Impact of Plant Closings" (press release), carried by U.S. Newswire on September 16, 2003.

9. "Trust Urges SEC Investigation of Briggs & Stratton; New 'Villain' Misled Investors or Duped Senators" (press release), carried by U.S. Newswire on September 17, 2003.

10. "Mower Engine Maker's Tactics on Hill Assailed," *Washington Post*, September 18, 2003.

11. Ibid.

12. Karen Kerrigan, "Could regulatory burden on small business disappear?" *Jacksonville Business Journal*, February 17, 2003; accessed at http://www.bizjournals.com/jacksonville/...s/2003/02/17/ editorial2.html?t=printable on Dec. 3, 2003.

13. United States Senate Committee on Small Business, press release, March 10, 1999.

14. Clyde Wayne Crews Jr., "The 10,000 Commandments," *Orange County Register*, July 13, 2003.

15. Ron Paul, "Economic Woes Begin at Home"; accessed at http://www.house.gov/paul/tst/tst2003/tst110303.htm on November 5, 2003.

16. Jeremy A. Leonard, "How Structural Costs Imposed on U.S. Manufacturers Harm Workers and Threaten Competitiveness," report prepared for the Manufacturing Institute of the National Association of Manufacturers, p. iii.

17. Ibid., pp. 2-3.

18. Ibid., p. 1.

19. Ibid., p. 19.

20. Quoted in Robert W. Lee, "A Bureaucratic Monster," *The New American*, September 21, 1992, p. 9.

21. Crews, p. 3.

22. Leonard, op. cit., p. 16.

23 Michael Fumento, American Economic Foundation newsletter (Volume V, Number 2).

24. Leonard, op. cit., p. 16.

25. Crews.

26. Ibid.

CHAPTER THREE — Amalgamating the Americas

1. "Palabras que sobra el tema 'Politica Exterior de Mexico en el Siglo XXI' que pronuncio el Presidente Vicente Fox" (Remarks on the theme, "Mexico's Foreign Policy for the 21st Century," as spoken by Mexican President Vicente Fox), transcription available on the Mexican government's website at http://www.presidencia.gob.mx/?P=42&Orden=Leer&Tipo=Art=3080; accessed on November 11, 2003.

2. William F. Jasper, "Gorbachev's Global Civil Society," *The New American*, October 9, 2000; Brzezinski's comments about "world government" and "regionalization" were transcribed

from a videotape of his address.

3. Quoted in Thomas R. Eddlem, "NAFTA: Bureaucracy Unlimited," *The New American*, October 18, 1993, pg. 19.

4. For a documented treatment of the role played by non-governmental organizations and "international civil society," see William F. Jasper, *The United Nations Exposed* (Appleton, Wis.: The John Birch Society, 2001), Chapter Five, "Orchestrating the Global Concert."

5. Benjamin Cohen, "Testimony on United States Trade Policies and Agricultural Disease: Safety, Economic, and Global Considerations," October 29, 1999; archived at http://www.cspinet.org/reports/sps_tes.html; accessed on November 4, 2003.

6. North American Commission for Environmental Cooperation website, http://www.cec.org/who_we_are?jpac/reports/1996/sec3_3.cfm?varlan=english; accessed on Nov. 4, 2003.

7. Eddlem, *The New American*.

8. " 'Free Trade' takes increasing hits," *Christian Science Monitor*, November 6, 2003.

9. "NAFTA's shop-floor impact," *Christian Science Monitor*, November 4, 2003.

10. Ibid.

11. Ibid.

12. Office of the U.S. Trade Representative, "Overview and the 2003 Agenda," p. 2.

13. "The Preparatory Process," statement on the official FTAA website, http://www.ftaa-alca.org/View_e.asp (1of5)10/28/2003; accessed on October 28, 2003.

14. Quoted in William P. Hoar, "The Great Sovereignty Sellout," *The New American*, December 13, 1993.

15. Nicole Anne Stubbs, "Regional Economic Integration: A Comparison of NAFTA and the EU," NAFTA Task Force Report 1998, archived at http://depts.washington.edu/canada/nafta/98chapters/4stubbsnafta98.htm; accessed on November 4, 2003.

CHAPTER FOUR — Caught in the WTO Web

1. Quoted in Jane H. Ingraham, "The Perfect Cover," *The New American*, August 13, 1991.

2. Richard Gardner, "The Hard Road to World Order," *Foreign Affairs*, April 1974, p. 558.

3. Reuters wire service story, November 10, 2003.

4. Ibid.

5. "U.S. Tariffs on Steel Are Illegal, World Trade Organization Says," *New York Times*, November 11, 2003.

6. Thomas R. Eddlem, "Our Sovereignty Trade-Away," *The New American*, December 26, 1994.

7. William F. Jasper, "Gingrich's Constitution Con," *The New American*, January 9, 1995.

8. Quoted in William P. Hoar, "Correction, Please!" *The New American*, November 28, 1994.

9. George W. Malone, *Mainline* (New Canaan, Conn.: The Long House, 1958), pp. 9-10.

10. Ibid., p. 7.

11. Ibid., pp. 25-26.

12. Ibid., p. 25.

13. Ibid., p. 35.

14. Ibid., p. 84.

15. Ibid., p. 19.

16. Ibid., pp. 18-19.

17. Patrick J. Buchanan, *The Great Betrayal: How American Sovereignty and Social Justice Are Being Sacrificed to the Gods of the Global Economy* (New York: Little, Brown and Company, 1998), p. 24.

18. Ibid., p. 25.

19. Malone, p. 30.

20. Eddlem, "Trading Away Our Sovereignty," *The New American*, March 7, 1994.

21. *Our Global Neighborhood: The Report of the Commission on Global Governance* (Oxford, England: Oxford University Press, 1995), pp. 167, 172.

22. Cited in William F. Jasper, "Trading Away Jobs and Liberty," *The New American*, June 30, 2003.

23. For a sample of the demands made by the European Union for access to American labor markets via GATS, see http://www. attac.org/fra/orga/doc/ue4us.htm.

24. Jasper, "Trading Away Jobs and Liberty."

25. Federation for American Immigration Reform, "Immigration and Trade Agreements," http://www.fairus.org/Immigration IssueCenters/Immigration IssueCenters.cfm?ID=2266&c=12; accessed on March 10, 2004.

26. Dan Stein, "Free Trade Deals Include Free Trade of Workers," op-ed column, September 15, 2003; accessed at http:// www.fairus/org/Media/Media.cfm?ID=416&c=35&insearch= chile on November 14, 2003.

CHAPTER FIVE — Electing a New People

1. Quoted in William R. Hawkins, *Importing Revolution: Open Borders and the Radical Agenda* (Monterey, Va.: The American Immigration Control Foundation, 1994), p. 103.

2. Quoted in Scott McConnell, "Americans No More?" *National Review*, December 31, 1997, p. 30.

3. President Bush address to Hispanic Chamber of Commerce, August 15, 2001; archived at http://www.whitehouse.gov/ news/releases/2001/08/print/20010815-3.html; accessed on December 1, 2003.

4. *Arizona Star*, "2004 entrant surge is under way," January 10, 2004; accessed at azstarnet.com on January 14, 2004.

5. "Border Patrol Union calls plan 'a slap in the face,'" San Diego *Union-Tribune*, January 13, 2004.

6. Ibid.

7. "Agents told to be silent on details of border plan," *Detroit Free Press*, January 21, 2004.

8. "Mexican leader applauds Bush's foreign-worker plan," *International Herald Tribune*, January 13, 2004; accessed at http://www.iht.com/cgi-bin/generic.cgi?template=arti-

cleprint.tmplh&ArticleId=124805 on February 4, 2004.

9. "President Bush Proposes New Temporary Worker Program: Remarks by the President on Immigration Policy"; accessed at http://www.whitehouse.gov/news/releases/2004/01/ 20040107-3.html on January 14, 2004.

10. Ibid.

11. Steve Sailer, interview with author.

12. "Coalition Provision Authority Request to Rehabilitate and Reconstruct Iraq," Baghdad, Iraq, September 2003, p. 3.

13. Ibid.

14. Ibid, pp. 8-9.

15. "Our Border Brigades," *Wall Street Journal*, January 27, 2004; accessed at http://www.opinionjournal.com/ forms/print-This.html?id=10004610 on February 2, 2004.

16. "The Illegal-Alien Crime Wave," Heather MacDonald, *City Journal*, Winter 2004; accessed at http://www.manhattan-institute.org/cfml/printable.cfm?id-1204 on February 3, 2004.

17. "Ex-Mexican consul arrested in connection with trafficking of illegal Arab migrants," San Diego *Union-Tribune*, November 13, 2003; accessed at http://www.sandiegocitysearch.com/ news/mexico/20031113-1553-mexico-ex-consularrested. html on February 4, 2004; "Smuggling case stokes new fears about Mexican border," *Chicago Tribune*, January 5, 2004; accessed at http://www.kentucky.com/mld/kentucky/news/ world/7640742.htm on February 4, 2004.

18. "Will Immigrants Harm America?" transcript of PBS television discussion program "Think Tank"; accessed at http://www.pbs. org/thinktank/transcript209.html on March 15, 2004.

19. William F. Jasper, "Bordering on Insanity," *The New American*, June 8, 1987.

20. William Norman Grigg, "Revolution in America," *The New American*, February 19, 1996.

21. Peter Brimelow, *Alien Nation: Common Sense About America's Immigration Disaster* (New York: HarperPerennial, 1995), pp. 76-77.

22. Ibid., p. 77.

23. Michael Lind, *The Next American Nation: The New National-ism and the Fourth American Revolution* (New York: Free Press, 1995), pp. 133-134.

24. The author spent considerable time living in Mexico and Guatemala, where he observed first-hand the admirable work ethic displayed by the people of those countries. His personal acquaintances include many Latinos — particularly from Mex-ico — whose capacity for honest labor is praiseworthy and wor-thy of emulation.

25. "Immigration: Boon or Bane to the U.S.? Red Ink from Abroad," by Donald Huddle and David Simcox, *World & I*, January 1994; accessed at http://www.worldandi.com/public/1994/january/mt3.cfm on March 10, 2004.

26. Victor Davis Hanson, *Mexifornia: A State of Becoming* (San Francisco: Encounter Books, 2003), p. 6.

27. Ibid., p. 21.

28. Ibid., pp. 7, 9, 12.

29. Ibid., p. 15.

30. Peter Brimelow, "Unnatural Disaster," *The American Conser-vative*, December 1, 2003, p. 26.

31. Hanson, pp. 15-16.

32. Ibid., pp. 18-19.

33. Jorge Castaneda, "Ferocious Differences," *Atlantic Monthly*, 1995, pp. 81-82.

34. *Washington Times*, August 13, 2001, pg. A-1; cited in Steve Sailer, "A Marshall Plan for Mexico"; accessed at http://www.vdare.com/sailer/marshall_plan.htm on March 10, 2004.

35. Allan Wall, "Undue Influence: The Government of Mexico and U.S. Immigration Policies," *The Social Contract*, Winter 2002-3, p. 95.

36. Ibid.

37. McConnell, p.30.

38. A very good capsule summary of the foundation-funded radi-cal Hispanic network is Joseph Fallon, "Funding Hate: Foun-

dations and the Radical Hispanic Lobby, Part 1," in *The Social Contract Quarterly*, Fall 2000; accessed at http://www.the socialcontract.com/cgi-bin/showarticle.pl?articleID=910& terms= on March 10, 2004.

39. Wall, p. 96.

40. Ibid., p. 97.

41. Ibid., p. 98.

42. Ibid., pp. 101-102.

43. "Remaking the Political Landscape: The Impact of Illegal and Legal Immigration on Congressional Apportionment," Dudley L. Poston Jr., Steven A. Camarota, and Amanda K. Baumle, Center for Immigration Studies, October 2003, pp. 1-2.

44. Ibid.

45. "Count on It," John J. Miller, *National Review*, December 8, 2003, p. 25.

46. A comprehensive review of the "Citizenship USA" scandal is found in David P. Schippers (with Alan P. Henry), *Sellout: The Inside Story of President Clinton's Impeachment* (Washington, D.C.: Regnery Publishing, 2000), pp. 37-49.

47. Howard Fineman, quoted in William Norman Grigg, "Abolishing Our Borders," *The New American*, October 8, 2001.

48. U.S.-Mexico Binational Commission, "Fact Sheet," http://dosfan.lib.uic.edu/ERC/bureaus/lat/1995/950509USMexicoBinational.html; accessed on December 1, 2003.

49. *Atlanta Journal-Constitution*, September 7, 2001, archived at http://www.americanpatrol.com/_WEBARCHIVES2000/web090801.html.

50. Ibid.

51. Ibid.

52. George W. Bush, comments to the press, August 24, 2001; accessed at http://www.whitehouse.gov/news/releases/2001/08/20010824.html on March 11, 2004.

53. *OPIC News*, June 2003.

54. "Towards à Partnership for Prosperity, The Guanajuato Proposal," Joint Communique issued by President George W. Bush

and President Vicente Fox, February 16, 2001; http://www.pres-idencia.gob.mx/?P=2&Orden=Leer&Tipo+Pe&Art=548; see also Dr. Raul Hinojosa Ojeda, et al., "Comprehensive Migration Policy Reform in North America: The Key to Sustainable and Equitable Economic Integration," North American Integration and Development Center, NAID Center Working Paper No. 12, August 29, 2001, p. 2, fn.

55. Ibid., p. 4.

56. "Our opinion: Bush's interest will help bill on guest-workers," *Tucson Citizen*, August 13, 2003.

57. "Immigrants ride for rights," *Atlanta Journal-Constitution*, September 30, 2003.

58. Immigrant Workers Freedom Ride website, http://www.iwfr.org/about.asp; accessed on October 3, 2003.

59. "Arizona lawmakers rally guest-worker supporters," Gannett News Service, November 20, 2003; accessed at http://www.az-central.com/p...come/news/articles/1120guestworker20.html on November 20, 2003.

60. "In N.M., Fox asks better health care, education for migrants," Associated Press, November 5, 2003; accessed at http://www.azcentral.com/p...al.com/news/articles/1105 FoxNM05-0N.html on November 19, 2003.

61. Robert D. Kaplan, *Warrior Politics: Why Leadership Demands a Pagan Ethos* (New York: Random House, 2002), pp. 137-138.

Chapter Six — What Can We Do?

1. George C. Lodge, *Managing Globalization in the Age of Interdependence* (San Diego: Pfeiffer & Company, 1995), p. 55.

2. Michael Hirsh, "The Death of a Founding Myth," Special Davos (International) Edition of *Newsweek*, December 2002-February 2002, p. 18.

3. Edmund Burke, *Thoughts on the Cause of the Present Discontent*, Vol. I, p. 526; accessed at http://www.bartleby.com/100/276.9.html on February 6, 2004.

4. *The State of Disunion Survey of American Political Culture*,

The Congressional Institute, archived at http://www. conginst.org/pulse/disunion/

5. Ibid., p. 9.

6. Ibid., p. 10.

7. Claire Sterling, *Octopus: The Long Reach of the International Sicilian Mafia* (London: W.W. Norton, 1990), p. 41.

8. Ibid., p. 42

9. Ibid., p. 42-43.

10. Ibid., p. 42.

11. Bernard Bailyn, *The Ideological Origins of the American Revolution* (Cambridge, Mass.; Harvard University Press, 1992), pp. xiii, 95.

12. John Locke, "An Essay Concerning the True Original extent, and end of, Civil Government," Book Two in *Great Books of the Western World*, Robert Maynard Hutchins, ed. (Chicago: Encyclopedia Britannica, 1952), vol. 35, p. 77.

13. Bailyn, p. 121.

14. Ibid., pp. 119-120.

15. Ibid., p. 321.

16. Carroll Quigley, *Tragedy and Hope: A History of the World in Our Time* (New York: The MacMillan Company, 1966), p. 950.

17. Ibid., pp. 1247-1248.

18. Christopher Lasch, *The Revolt of the Elites and the Betrayal of Democracy* (New York: W.W. Norton & Company, 1995), pp. 25-26.

19. Ibid., p. 45.

APPENDIX I — Descent into Degeneracy

1. The Marquis de Sade, *Juliette*, Austryn Wainhouse, trans. (New York: Grove Weidenfeld, 1968), p. 68.

2. Interview with Marilyn Manson conducted by "Anal Retentive," transcription at http://theophobia.tripod.com/c-4pi4p. htm; accessed on October 22, 2003.

3. Gabriel Garcia Marquez, "The Mysteries of Bill Clinton," *Salon*, February 1, 1999; archived at http://www.salon.com/

news/1999/02/cov_02news.html; accessed on Oct. 22, 2003.

4. Michael Novak, "A Half-Witted NFL?" National Review Online, February 4, 2004; accessed at http://www.national review.com/script/printpage.asp?ref=/novak/novak2004 02040848.asp on February 4, 2004.

5. Sally Jenkins, "NFL Exposed For What It Is," *Washington Post*, February 3, 2004.

6. "Viewers' favorite ads crude, rude and furry," *USA Today*, February 2, 2004.

7. Ibid.

8. "The Lost Children of Rockdale County," PBS *Frontline*, October 19, 1999; transcript accessed at wysiwyg://331/http://www.pbs.org/wgbh/pages/frontline/shows/georgia/etc/script.html on October 28, 2003; p. 2.

9. Ibid., p. 3.

10. Ibid., pp. 3-4, 7.

11. Ibid., p. 7.

12. Ibid.

13. Bob Herbert, "An Ugly Game," *New York Times*, October 17, 2003.

14. "Lost Children" transcript, pp. 24-25.

15. Ibid., p. 4.

16. Ibid., p. 1.

17. Richard Grenier, *Capturing the Culture*, (Washington: Ethics & Public Policy Center, 1991).

18. Carroll Quigley, *Tragedy and Hope: A History of the World in Our Time* (New York: MacMillan Co., 1966), pp. 1245, 1248.

19. Ibid., p. 1249.

20. Ibid., p. 1250.

21. Ibid., pp. 1251-1252.

22. Ibid., p. 1252.

23. Ibid.

24. Ibid.

25. Col. Ronald D. Ray, USMC (Ret.), "Kinsey's Legal Legacy," *The New American*, January 19, 1998.

26. In a PBS interview, Jones explained: "Kinsey [was] at odds with the way society regulates human sexual behavior, and what he [wanted] to see is a much more encompassing ethic of tolerance that will make room at the table for lots of different kinds of people who don't fit under the cookie cutters of prescribed morality." He also admits that Kinsey's "desire to change how people view human sexual behavior," which was "so embedded in his being," led him to conclude that "if the information is presented with the right complexion then it will allow only one set of conclusions, which is in the direction of social tolerance.... What Kinsey did, I think, was to make behavior that seemed very marginal but aberrant in a moral lexicon much more common and much more approachable to people because he says it represents X amount of the population." He also has described Kinsey's "homo-erotic interest.... [He was] attracted to members of the same sex sexually, and beginning certainly by the late 1930s, he is beginning to try to explore and act upon his private needs." This was a reluctant and grudging validation of the charge that Kinsey's "research" was done in the service of his own personal and revolutionary agenda. Accessed at http://www.pbs.org/fmc/interviews/jones.htm on March 11, 2004.

27. Dr. Judith A. Reisman and Edward W. Fichel, with Dr. John H. Court and Dr. J. Gordon Muir, eds., *Kinsey, Sex and Fraud: The Indoctrination of a People* (Lafayette, La.; Lochinvar-Huntington House, 1990), p. 6, fn.

28. Quoted in ibid., p. 6.

29. Ibid., p. 8.

30. Judith A. Reisman, Ph.D., *"Soft Porn" Plays Hardball* (Lafayette, La.: Huntington House Publishers, 1991), p. 35.

31. Ibid.

32. Ibid., p. 41.

33. Quoted in "Hef's Baby: Playboy's abortion activism plays out," Paul Belien, *American Conservative*, February 2, 2004, p. 17.

34. Ibid., p. 18.

35. Andrew Stuttaford, "Played Out? The magazine that Hef built,

at 50," National Review Online, December 2003; wysi-wyg://496/http://www.nationalreview.com/stuttaford/stuttaford.asp; accessed on February 4, 2004; Catherine Seipp, "Living with *Playboy*: It ain't all bad," National Review Online, January 13, 2004; wysiwyg://489/http://www.nationalreview.com/comment/seipp200401130854.asp; accessed on Feb. 4, 2004.

36. Seipp.

37. Eric Schlosser, *Reefer Madness: Sex, Drugs, and Cheap Labor in the American Black Market* (Boston: Houghton Mifflin, 2003), p. 185.

38. Ibid., pp 186-187.

39. Ibid., p. 188.

40. Ibid., p. 186.

41. Kingsley Davis, quoted in Robert Whelan, *Choices in Childbearing* (London: The Committee on the Population & The Economy, 1992), p. 4.

42. Ibid., pp 54-55.

43. Schlosser, p. 178.

44. "What's Going On? Notes on the Right Turn," Michael Walzer, *Dissent*, January 1996, p. 7.

45. Ibid., p. 6.

46. Roland Huntford, *The New Totalitarians* (New York: Stein and Day, 1971), p. 326.

APPENDIX II — The Wages of Perpetual War

1. "Back to the Womb? Isolationism's Renewed Threat," *Foreign Affairs*, July/August 1995, p. 8.

2. "The Reservist's Unexpected War," *Washington Post*, July 28, 2003.

3. "The Army be thuggin' it," *Salon*, October 17, 2003.

4. The best study of the long-term campaign to subvert our armed forces is *Changing Commands: The Betrayal of America's Military*, by former Marine officer John F. McManus (Appleton, Wis.: The John Birch Society, 1995).

5. On the day after the 9-11 attack, President Bush and British

Prime Minister Tony Blair agreed that military reprisals against Afghanistan and other terrorist-sponsoring states would require NATO and UN approval; see Bob Woodward and Dan Balz, "We Will Rally the World," *Washington Post*, January 28, 2002; archived at http://www.btinternet.com/~nlpwessex/Documents/WashingtonPost28Jan.htm; accessed on March 11, 2004.

6. On scores of occasions, President Bush explicitly said that the purpose of the U.S.-led invasion of Iraq was to enforce UN arms control decrees and enhance the world body's credibility. A good selection of specific quotes, complete with specific citations, can be found at http://www.thenewamerican.com/tna/2003/06-30-2003/vo19no13_delusion.htm.

7. Regarding the role played by the U.S. government and its allies in building up and supporting Saddam Hussein's regime, see: Peter Mantius, *Shell Game: A True Story of Banking, Spies, Lies, Politics — and the Arming of Saddam Hussein* (New York: St. Martin's Press, 1995); Alan Friedman, *Spider's Web* (New York: Bantam Books, 1992); and Kenneth Timmerman, *Death Lobby: How the West Armed Iraq* (New York: Houghton Mifflin, 1991). See also the very useful on-line compendium of documented exposés archived at http://www.thenewamerican.com/focus/iraq/index.htm.

8. The clearest exposition of George W. Bush's plans for a global "democratic revolution" was offered in his February 26, 2003 address to the American Enterprise Institute, the text of which is archived at http://www.whitehouse. gov/news/releases/2003/02/20030226-11.html; accessed on March 11, 2004.

9. Thomas P.M. Barnett, "The Pentagon's New Map: It Explains Why We're Going to War, and Why We'll Keep Going to War," *Esquire*, March 2003; accessed at http://192.168.0.254/dsc-gi/ds.py/cet/fil...quire_story_&_details_about_Barnett).htm on December 2, 2003.

10. Ibid.

11. Ibid.

12. Ibid.

13. Ibid.

14. "Thomas Barnett 'Live' with TAE," *The American Enterprise*, December 2003, p. 14.

15. Ibid., p. 16

16. "Back to the Womb? Isolationism's Renewed Threat," *Foreign Affairs*, July/August 1995, p. 8.

17. "Toll on U.S. Troops grows as wounded rolls approach 10,000," *Orlando Sentinel*, November 28, 2003.

18. Ibid.

19. "For Citizen Soldiers, an Unexpected Burden," *New York Times*, September 15, 2003.

20. "Protests Grow over Year-Long Army Tours," *Washington Post*, September 20, 2003.

21. Ibid.

22. Gannett News Service, November 27, 2003.

23. "The Hearts Left Behind," by Jerry Adler, *Newsweek*, November 17, 2003; archived at http://msnbc.msn.com/id/3403522/; accessed on March 11, 2004.

24. Ibid.

25. "Mom who won't return to Iraq taken off active duty," Colorado Springs *Gazette*; accessed at http://www.gazette.com/display. php?sid= 665566 on December 2, 2003.

26. "AWOL Mom Can Stay in U.S., But…," CBS News, November 11, 2003; http://www.cbsnews.com/stories/2003/11/10/ iraq accessed on December 2, 2003.

27. Bill Kauffman, "An Empire of Widows and Orphans: George Bush, the Anti-Family President," CounterPunch, October 27, 2003; http://www.counterpunch.org/kauffman10272003. html accessed on December 2, 2003.

28. Ibid.

29. "Army Reserve fears troop exodus," *USA Today,* Sept. 30, 2003.

30. "Army, National Guard to evolve for speed," *Charlotte Observer*, September 18, 2003.

31. "Some reservists ponder quitting as service time grows," Milwaukee *Journal Sentinel*, September 13, 2003.

Index

Accenture, 11
"Adam & Eve" catalog, 121
Adams, John, 97
A Family of One, 134
Afghanistan, 127
Africa, 73
Agriculture, Department of, 24
AIDS, 119
Alaska, 45
Albuquerque, New Mexico, 64
al-Qaeda, 127
American Association of Sex
    Educators, Counselors, and
    Therapists, 121
American Bar Association, 117
American Civil Liberties Union
    (ACLU), 117
American Express, 14
American Legal Institute (ALI),
    117
American Revolution, 97
*American Sexual Behavior and
    the Kinsey Report*, 116
American Textile Manufacturers
    Institute, 3
anti-Christian, 106
anti-Jewish, 106
Argentineans, 19
Arizona Star, 64
Arizona, 64
Arlacchi, Pino, 94
Armed Forces, 126
Asia, 19, 67, 73
Atlanta Journal-Constitution,
    84, 88
Atlanta, 80

Atlantic Monthly, 123
Austin, Texas, 14
Australia, 129
Aztlan, 79

Badger Tech Metals, 2
Bailyn, Bernard, 96
Bangalore, India, 12
Bank of America, 12
Barnett, Thomas P.M., 128, 131
Barr, Bob, 82
Beijing, 9
Belize, 77
Bell, Daniel, 94
Bender, Jay, 8
Benjamin, Harry, 116
Bennett, Jimmy and/or Verleen,
    2, 3
Bennett, Robert, 5
Berelson Memorandum, 122
Berelson, Bernard, 122
Berges, James, 28
Bible Belt, 111
bin Laden, Osama, 126
Black Tuesday (9-11), 68, 87,
    126-127, 129
Blazar, Ernie, 26
Bond, Kit, 26
Bonner, T.J., 64
Border Environment Coopera-
    tion Commission, 84
Border Patrol Council, 64
Border Patrol, 64
Boston, 11, 132
Boughader, Salim, 70
Brandeis, Louis, 117

Brave New World, 124
Brecht, Berthold, 63
Bremer, Charles, 3
Brennan, William J., 117
Bretton Woods Conference, 54
Briggs & Stratton, 24-26
Brimelow, Peter, 71, 73
Britain, 29
British Crown, 97
Brod, Andrew, 6
Brookings, South Dakota, 8, 135
Brussels, 46
Brzezinski, Zbigniew, 35
Buckley, William F., Jr., 120
Burke, Edmund, 91
Bush (I) administration, 122
Bush, George W., 4, 35-37, 48,
    63-71, 78, 83-88, 122, 126-
    128, 131

Caldwell, Taylor, 1, 20
California Air Resources Board
    (CARB), 25
California National Guard, 132
California, 11, 27, 58, 74-75
Canada, 29, 41, 83-85
Canton, Ohio, 1
*Carey v. Population Services In-
    ternational*, 118
Caribbean, 73, 75
Carnegie Foundation, 117
Carolina Panthers, 107
Carter, Jimmy, 89
Castaneda, Jorge, 77
CATO Institute, 30
Center for Immigration Reform,
    82
Center for Science in the Public
    Interest (CSPI), 39
Central America, 36, 67
Chastain, Roger, 1

ChevronTexaco, 11-12
Chicago Tribune, 83
Chicago's Crime Commission,
    94
Chicano, 75
China Design Centre, 13
China, 2, 11, 13, 29, 129
Chinese, 8
Choate, Pat, 10
Christian Science Monitor, 14
Church of Satan, 105
Cicero, 23
CIO Magazine, 12
Citizenship USA program, 83
Civil War, 59
Clarke, Jeff, 13
Clear Air Trust, 26
Clinton administration, 82
Clinton, Bill, 98, 105
Club XXI, 35
Cohen, Benjamin, 39-40
Cold War, 44, 130
Colombia, 88
Colorado, 79
Columbia University, 47, 117
Columbine, 111
Commission on Global Gover-
    nance, 57
Communist, 111
Communist China, 3, 37
Communist Party, U.S.A., 88
Congress, 27, 34, 53
Constitution, U.S., 1, 33, 97, 130
Conyers, Georgia, 108
Cooper, Peggy, 109
Council on Foreign Relations
    (CFR), 44
coyotes, 64-65
Credit Lyonnais Securities, 19
Crews, Clyde Wayne, Jr., 30
Crudele, John, 4

Customs and Border Protection, 65
Cutler, Mike, 65

Davis, Kingsley, 122
Davis, Mike, 63
"Death of a Founding Myth, The," 91
Declaration of Human Rights, 54
Declaration of Independence, 97
"Declaration of Principles," 35
Dell Computer, 10, 14
Democrat, 25
Democrats, 99
Transportation, Department of 24
Deutsch, Donny, 107
developing world, 52
Dickinson, Robert, 116
Disney Toys, 14
Dissent, 123
divorce, 119
Doe v. Bolton, 118
Dole, Bob, 50
Draut, Tamara, 16
drug use and addiction, 119
Dumbarton Oaks, 54

East Asia, 4
East Coast, 11
East Germany, 83
Econ 101, 67
economic deterrents/incentives, 122
Eddlem, Thomas R., 40
Eden, Barbara, 113
Eisenstadt v. Baird, 118
Electoral College, 82
"El Embajador of Mexico," 67
Emerson, 28

Emory University School of Public Health, 108
Emory University, 85
England, 83
Enlightenment, 123
Enron, 27
Environmental Protection Agency, 24, 32
Equal Employment Opportunity Commission, 80
Ernst, Morris, 116
European Union (EU), 20, 33, 45-46, 52, 59, 84, 129
Excelsior, 79
Export Import Bank of the US, 86

Fabian socialists, 112
Falcon Plastics, 8
Family Planning Perspectives, 122
Farewell Address, 114
FBI, 83
FCC, 107
Federal Register, 28
Federal Reserve, 4
Federation for American Immigration Reform, 59
Feinstein, Dianne, 26
50 Cent., 109-110
Fineman, Howard, 83
Flake, Jeff, 87-88
Flanagan, Kevin, 12
Florida, 81
Ford Foundation, 79, 81, 121
Forrester Research, 14
Founders (American), 95, 97, 101
Founding Fathers, 126
Fox, Vicente, 35, 66, 80, 84, 89, 90

France, 10, 29
Frankfurter, Felix, 117
Frecker, John, 64
Free Trade Area of the Americas
     (FTAA), 35-38, 45-46, 89,
     102
Free Trade Council, 40
Fumento, Michael, 32
"Functioning Core" nations,
     129-130
furniture industry, 6

Gardner, Richard, 47
Garza, Tony, 67
GATS (General Agreement on
     Trade in Services), 57, 58-59
GATT (General Agreement on
     Tariffs and Trade), 47, 53, 57
GDP (Gross Domestic Product),
     57
Gearhart, Bertrand, 56
Geneva, 48, 59
Genocide Convention, 54
George C. Lodge, 91
George Mason University, 43
Georgetown University, 98, 112
Georgia State University, 85
Georgia, 80, 84
Germany, 10, 23, 29
Gingrich, Newt, 50-51
"Global South," 52
God, 105
Goheen, John, 137
Golden State, 58
Gomorrah, 111
Gonzalez, Jorge, 41
Gorbachev, Mikhail, 45
Gore, Al, 82
Gorski, Mike, 132
Gramsci, Antonio, 111, 115
Grassley, Charles, 48

Great Britain, 46, 95, 97, 126
Greathouse, Jim, 1
Greek, 75
Greenspan, Alan, 4
Greenville, South Carolina, 2
Grenier, Richard, 111
Griswold v. Connecticut, 118
Guatemala, 77, 83
Guyon, Rene, 116

H-1B visas, 11, 59
Haiti, 14
Hand, Learned, 117
Hanson, Victor Davis, 75
Harvard Business School, 91
Harvard, 53
Harvey, Philip, 120-122
Havana, 55
Hayward, California, 132
Hazard Emergency Response
     Act (1986), 32
Hefner, Hugh, 118-120
Helmly, James, 135
Herbert, Bob, 109-110
Hermosillo, Mexico, 64
Hesburgh, Theodore, 89
heterophobia, 119
Hillsborough, North Carolina,
     120
Hirsh, Michael, 91
Hispanic Chamber of Com-
     merce, 63-64
Hiss, Alger, 55
Hitler, Adolf, 23,
Hitlerian, 106
Hobbes, Thomas, 114
Holcomb, Simone, 135
Holcomb, Vaughn, 135
Hong Kong, 19
Hooker Furniture Corporation,
     5, 6

Hoover vacuum factory, 1
Hotel Eurobuilding, 35
House of Representatives, 81
House Ways and Means Committee, 51
Housing and Urban Development, Department of, 24
housing policies, 122
Houston, 80
Huddle, Donald, 74
Human Biodiversity Institute, 67
Huntford, Roland, 124
Huntsman, Jon M., 23
Hussein, Saddam, 127, 129, 131
Huxley, Aldous, 124

"I Dream of Jeanie," 113-114
IMF, 102
Immigrant Workers Freedom Ride, 88
Immigration Reform and Control Act of 1986 (IRCA), 65, 89
impotence and homosexuality, 119
India, 3, 10, 129
Indian, 75
Indiana, 47, 81
Indonesia, 14
INS, 83
Integnology Corp, 14
Interior, Department of, 24
International Bank and Fund, 54
International Monetary Fund (IMF), 55
International Trade Organization (ITO), 48, 55-56
Iraq, 68, 88, 127, 132-133, 135
Iraqi Provisional Authority, 69
Isthmus of Tehuantepec, 77
Italy, 111

Jackson, Janet, 106
Jaffe, Frederic, 122
Jamaica, 36
Janjua, Basheer, 14
Japan, 29, 129
Japanese, 8
Jasper, William F., 13
Jefferson, Thomas, 49, 97, 99
Jenkins, Sally, 107
John Birch Society, The, 101-102
Joint Economics Committee, 5
Joint Public Advisory Committee (of NACEC), 40
Jones, James H., 116
Judeo-Christian, 115
just war, 125
Justice Department, 121

Kannapolis, North Carolina, 2-3
Kantor, Mickey, 38
Kaplan, Robert D., 90
Kaufman, Bill, 135-136
Kay, David, 127
Kefauver, Estes, 94
Kemp, Jack, 49
Kennedy, Edward, 72
Kennedy, Robert F., 72
Kentucky, 81
Keokuk, Iowa, 56
Kernersville, North Carolina, 6-7
Kid Rock, 106
King, Martin Luther, Jr., 88
Kinsey, Alfred C., 115-119
Kinslow, Eric, 135
Kissinger, Henry, 44
Kohl, Herbert, 25
Kolbe, Jim, 87-88
Ku Klux Klan, 88

L-1 visa program, 11, 59
La Cosa Nostra, 94, 120
La Raza, 75
La Reconquista, 77, 79
Labor Day, 4
Labor, Department of, 76
Lasch, Christopher, 100
Latin America, 73, 75
Latin, 75
League of Nations, 56
League of United Latin American Citizens (LULAC), 67, 80
Lebanon, 70
Lessin, Nancy, 132
Leviathan, 114
Libertarian, 118
Lind, Michael, 73
Locke, John, 96, 100
London Guardian, 128
London, 128
Lord of the Flies, 109
Loret de Mola, Carlos, 63, 79
Los Angeles Times, 44
Lynch, Jessica, 135
Lynn, Barry, 10

Maastricht, 52
Madeiros, Justin, 125
Madison, James, 31, 58, 71, 125, 126, 137
Madrid, Spain, 35
Mafia, 94-95, 98, 100, 120
Magnequench, 9-10
Mahmoud Abouhalima, 70
Malaysians, 19
Malone, George W., 53-55
man, 105
Manson, Marilyn, 105
March, Louis T., 15
Marquis de Sade, 105, 123

Marxism, 112
Marxist, 63, 112, 116, 123, 130
Marxist-Leninist, 130
matricula consular cards, 70
Maus, Teodoro, 80
Mayberry, 111
McCain, John, 87-88
McCarran-Walter Act, 72
McCoy, John C., 7-8
McFerran, Warren L., 31
McKiever, Jeanean, 134
Menomonee, Wisconsin, 2
Mesopotamian, 69
Mexicana (airlines), 64
Mexican-American Legal Defense and Education Fund (MALDEF), 80-81
Mexican-American, 75
Mexican-Anglo, 85
Mexico City, 87
Mexico, 4, 9, 29-30, 38, 41, 43, 63-64, 67, 70-71, 73-75, 77-81, 83-90
"Mexifornia," 74
Miami, 35
Michigan, 81
middle class, 1-2, 7, 10, 17, 19-20, 43, 46, 61, 92, 98-99, 112-115, 122, 130
Middle East, 54, 70, 127
Miller v. California, 118
Miller, Edward, 10
Miller, John J., 82
Milwaukee, 137
Mises, Ludwig von, 23
Mississippi, 81
Model Penal Code, 117
Molotov, V.M., 55
Montana, 81
Monterrey, Mexico, 86
moon, 15

Morrow, Robert, 18
Moscow, 127
Mount Vernon Mills, 1
Movimiento Estudiantil de Chicanos de Aztlan (MEChA), 80
MTV, 106-107, 110
Mussolini, Benito, 111

Nader, Ralph, 39
NAFTA, 30, 38-45, 52, 57-58, 61, 84, 89
NAM, 32
National Association of Manufacturers (NAM), 28
National Council for Mexicans Abroad, 80
National Council of La Raza, 80
National Defense magazine, 10
National Foreign Trade Council, 56
National Guard, 136-137
National Guard Association, 137
National Lawyers Guild, 117
National Review, 120
National Security Adviser, 35
National Socialism, 19
National Socialist Party, 23
Nelly, 109
Nelson, Bill, 133
Nelson, Bret, 15
Nevada, 53
New Deal, 59
New Delhi, 14
New England Patriots, 106
New School for Social Research, 45
New York City, 45, 88, 120
New York Post, 4
New York Times, 79
New York (state), 81-82

New Zealand, 130
Newsweek, 83, 91
NFL, 107
Nickerson, Thomas, 125
Nike, 14
9-11, 68, 87, 126-127, 129 (see also, "Black Tuesday")
1996 Summer Olympics, 108
Noel, Cynthia, 109
"Non-Integrating Gap" nations, 129-130
North America, 129
North American Commission for Environmental Cooperation (NACEC), 40
North American Development Bank (NADBank), 38, 84
North American Financial Group (NAFG), 38
North American Free Trade Agreement (NAFTA), 38-39, 44-45
North Korea, 78
Novak, Michael, 106

Occupational Safety and Health Administration, 24
Ohio, 4
Oklahoma, 81
Omnitech Technical Associates, 7
Organization for American States (OAS), 35
Ortiz Abdala, Imelda, 70
Our Global Neighborhood, 57
Overseas Private Investment Corporation (OPIC), 86

Pakistan, 3
Palermo, Sicily, 94
Panama City, Florida, 110

Partnership for Prosperity (PfP), 85-87
PBS *Frontline*, 108
Pennsylvania, 81
Pentagon, 129
Permanent Normal Trade Relations (PNTR), 9
Perot, H. Ross, 27
Persian Gulf, 128
Peters, Jamie, 134
Peterson, Virgil, 94
Pettengill, Samuel B., 47
PHE, Inc., 121
Philippines, 14
Piestewa, Lori, 135
Pillowtex, 2
Planned Parenthood of America, 117
Planned Parenthood, 122
Playboy Channel, 109, 118
Playboy, 118-119
Pleasant Hill, California, 133
Pomeroy, Wardell, 116
Population Council, 122
Population Services International, 120
Preciado, Felipe de Jesus, 77
Preston, Anita, 133
Preston, Jory, 133
PriceWaterhouseCoopers, 11
Prison Notebooks, 111
Prisoners of the American Dream, 63
Proposition 187, 80
Puritan, 114
Putin, Vladimir, 129

Quigley, Carroll, 98-99, 112-113

Reagan administration, 121-122
Reagan, Ronald, 32

Reconstruction, 59
Red Tape Reduction Act, 27
Reding, Andrew, 45
Reece, Carroll, 115
Reefer Madness, 123
Reisman, Judith, 118
Report on Male Sexuality, 116
Republicans, 99
Revolutionary War, 50
Rice University, 74
Richebacher, Kurt, 16-17
Roberts, Paul Craig, 11, 53
Roberts, Russell, 43
Rockdale County, Georgia, 108, 110-111, 118
Rockefeller Foundation, 117
Rockefeller, David, 44, 122
Rockefellers, 116
Roe v. Wade, 118
Roman, 23
Roosevelt, Franklin D., 53
Rumsfeld, Donald, 128
Russia, 10, 78, 129
Russians, 19

Sacramento State University, 11
Sailer, Steve, 67-68
Salameh, Mohammed, 70
San Antonio, 41
San Diego, 64
San Francisco, 54, 123
San Joaquin Valley, 76
San Ramon, California, 11
San Ysidro, California, 64
Satan, 105
Savage, Thomas, 25
Save our American Manufacturing (SAM), 7
Schlesinger, Arthur, Jr. , 125, 131
Schlosser, Eric, 121-123
"seam states," 129-130

SEATO, 54
Second Treatise on Government, 96
Secretary of Housing and Urban Development, 49
Secretary of State, 44
Securities and Exchange Commission (SEC), 26
Selma, California, 76
Senate Finance Committee, 48
Senate Majority Leader, 50
Senate Military Affairs Committee, 54
Sex Information and Education Council of the United States (SIECUS), 117
Sexual Behavior in the Human Male, 116
Shays, Christopher, 134
Sheth, Jagdish, 85
Shirer, William, 23
Sjoquist, David, 85
Skoff, Jerry, 2, 7
social constraints, 122
social controls, 122
Soong, Daniel, 11-12
South Africa, 130
South America, 36, 129
South Korea, 29, 32
Southwestern United States, 63
Soviet Union, 75
Speaker of the House, 50
St. Augustine, 95
St. Louis, 28, 110
State Department (Agency for International Development), 121
Stein, Dan, 59
Sterk, Claire, 108
Sterling, Claire, 95
Stiles, Mildred, 6

Stubbs, Nicole Anne, 45
suicide, 119
Summit of the Americas, 35
Super Bowl Sunday, 105
Super Bowl XXXVIII, 108-110
Super Bowl, 107, 109
Supreme Court, 117-118
Sweden, 124

Taiwan, 29
Tennessee, 84
Tennyson, 66
Texas, 10, 79
"Texicans," 83
textile industry, 6
The City of God, 95
The Congressional Institute, 93
The Federalist Papers, 31
The Foundation 1000, 81
The Immigration Reform Act (IRA) of 1965, 72
The Lost Children of Rockdale County, 108
The New American, 13
The New Totalitarians, 124
The State of Disunion, 93
Third Reich, 23
Third World, 52
Tierra del Fuego, 45
Timberlake, Justin, 106
Time magazine, 14
Toms, Paul, 6
Trade Adjustment Assistance program, 43
Trade Agreements Act of 1934, 54-55
Tragedy and Hope, 98, 112
Transportation, Department of, 24
Treasury, Department of, 10, 24, 53

Treaty of Guadalupe Hidalgo 79
Tribe, Lawrence, 53
Trilateral Commission, 35, 44
Trinity University, 41

U.S. Army, 136
U.S. Army Reserve, 136-137
U.S. Army Accessions Command, 125
U.S. Border Patrol, 64-65
U.S. Chamber of Commerce, 56
U.S. Congress, 49, 52
U.S. Constitution, 49
U.S. Department of Labor, 80
U.S. Military, 130
U.S. Naval War College, 129
U.S. State Department, 86
U.S. Trade Representative, 38, 57, 59
U.S.-Mexico Binational Commission, 84
UNESCO, 54
United Nations (UN), 21, 45-46, 53, 102, 128, 131
United Nations Charter, 35
United States Marines, 132
United States of America, 4, 23, 29, 48, 85, 90, 92-91, 101
University of North Carolina-Chapel Hill, 121
University of Washington, 45
UNRRA (United Nations Relief and Relocation Agency), 54
US Trade and Development Agency, 86
USA Today, 16
Utah, 5, 81

Valparaiso, Indiana, 9
venereal disease, 119
Vietnam, 3

Vitale, Leonardo, 94

Wagnerian, 106
Wall Street Journal, 3, 68-69, 76
Wall, Alan, 78
Walzer, Michael, 123
Washington Post, 2, 84
Washington, 7
Washington, D.C., 33, 35-36, 86, 127- 128
Washington, George, 114
Watson, Peter S., 86
Wechsler, Herbert, 117
Western Hemisphere, 20
White House, 48, 84
Whitehall Palace, 128
Wichita, Kansas, 56
Wisconsin, 7, 24-25, 81
Wood, Christopher, 19
Working Group on Emergency Actions (of Free Trade Council), 40-41
World Affairs Council, 35
World Bank, 36, 55, 102
World Trade Center, 70
World Trade Organization (WTO), 21, 45, 50-51, 53, 56, 58, 130-131
World Trade Organization, Appellate Body, 48
World War I, 59
World War II, 135

About the Author

An award-winning investigative journalist, William Norman Grigg is Senior Editor for *The New American* magazine.

As a correspondent for *The New American*, Mr. Grigg has covered numerous United Nations summits and conferences, including the 1994 population control summit in Cairo, Egypt, the 1995 social development summit in Copenhagen, Denmark, and the 2000 Millennium Forum and 2001 small arms conference, both at UN Headquarters in New York City.

Mr. Grigg has written and co-produced several video documentaries, including *Tragedy by Design* (1997), *Injustice for All: The International Criminal Court* (1998), and *Civilian Disarmament: Prelude to Tyranny* (2000).

Much in demand as a speaker, Mr. Grigg has addressed live audiences nationwide, has been featured as a guest on numerous talk shows, and appeared on C-SPAN.

His previous books are *The Gospel of Revolt: Feminism vs. The Family* (1993), *Freedom on the Altar: The UN's Crusade Against God and Family* (1995), and *Global Gun Grab: The United Nations Campaign to Disarm Americans* (2001).

Mr. Grigg resides in Appleton, Wisconsin with his wife Korrin and their children William, Isaiah, Jefferson, and Katrina.

About the Author

Recommended Action

Having read *America's Engineered Decline*, you can now appreciate the urgency to activate Congress to stop the FTAA. The John Birch Society invites you to visit our STOP the FTAA website at **www.stoptheftaa.org** and join with thousands of other concerned Americans who want to keep their country free and independent and preserve the unique opportunities that have made America great.

Building informed constituent pressure is the key to convincing Congress to stand up to the globalist agenda and vote against any agreement that would set up an FTAA. The *STOP the FTAA Starter Packet* ($9.95 + shipping & handling) contains materials and plans that will help you become an effective participant in this battle. Together, following an organized program, we can make a difference.

America's Engineered Decline

is available in single or discounted quantities.

Quantity	Price/Book*
1	$5.95
10	$4.95
50	$3.95
100+	$3.78

Order online at **www.stoptheftaa.org**
or call **1-800-JBS-USA1**
or write to:

STOP the FTAA
P.O. Box 8040
Appleton, WI 54912

*Please add Shipping and Handling:

Order Subtotal	Standard Shipping	Rush Shipping
$0–$10.99	$3.95	$8.95
$11.00-$19.99	$6.75	$11.75
$20.00–$49.99	$8.95	$13.95
$50.00–$99.99	$11.75	$16.75
$100.00-$149.99	$13.95	$18.95
$150.00+	call	call

Standard: 4-14 business days.
Rush: 3-7 business days, no P.O. boxes. Alaska/Hawaii, add $10.00

Wisconsin residents add 5% sales tax to all orders.